E. A Maling

Song Birds

How To Keep Them

E. A Maling

Song Birds
How To Keep Them

ISBN/EAN: 9783744767866

Printed in Europe, USA, Canada, Australia, Japan

Cover: Foto ©Andreas Hilbeck / pixelio.de

More available books at **www.hansebooks.com**

SONG BIRDS

SONG BIRDS,

AND

HOW TO KEEP THEM.

By E. A. MALING,

AUTHOR OF "IN-DOOR PLANTS, AND HOW TO GROW THEM,"
AND "FLOWERS AND FOLIAGE FOR IN-DOOR PLANTS."

WITH A FRONTISPIECE.

LONDON:
SMITH, ELDER AND CO., 65, CORNHILL,

M.DCCC.LXII.

PREFACE.

In writing this little book for the use of those who, like myself, are fond of birds, and anxious to make their lives among us as joyous as their songs, I do not set myself up to be a scientific birdkeeper. My own birds have thriven and become extremely tame, and they seem as happy as little birds can be; yet mine professes to be simply a natural mode of treatment. My experience of birds' ways began when a child, in becoming familiar with them while in their wild state, and I have since gone on gathering from books, and friends, and personal observations, details of their habits when free; thus learning how to make them more happy in confinement.

Judging in some degree by what my own wants have been, I hope that this book may be of use to others; and it shall be at least kept free from several topics which render many bird books really painful reading.

Bird-trapping, for instance, bird-doctoring in many cases, and the usual ways of so-called bird-taming, are not ladies' works; indeed, instructions on such points always seem to me of little use to any one. My own belief is, that it is very easy to tame birds by kindness, and to keep them in health by cleanliness and warmth, with plenty of fresh air and only simple food; while few mistresses, I am sure, would wish to teach amusing tricks to their little pets by means of fear or hunger, or to torment them when sick by trying, with unskilful and trembling hands, to administer remedies which are almost always useless, and very often painful to such fragile patients.

The real art of taming is very little dwelt on in bird books; yet this is generally the first object of those who keep such pets. In writing of this subject, I fear I have been tempted to record too many of my own birds' doings; though I hope this may be forgiven me, on the ground that as a good novel gives the best insight into the manners of a country, so a relation of what actually goes on under any course of treatment is often the best explanation of it.

While, then, I confess to having no pretensions to the science of ornithology, my own fondness for birds has led me to read the works and to test the advice of many of the best authorities on the subject, comparing it with what I have seen of the birds themselves; and as during some time, illness has reduced me to the companionship of birds for much of my chief amusement, the numbers that fill my room have made me very familiar with many of their ways.

I have, therefore, tried to show in this little volume how birds may be made tame, and how easily they may be kept; hoping that it may help in opening out to many a very great source of interest : while, at the same, time it may aid in rendering the treatment of birds more natural, and in making them more happy, when we, for our pleasure, keep them in confinement.

Whitehead's Grove, Chelsea,
    Sept. 24*th*, 1861.

CONTENTS.

————

Contents.

SONG BIRDS,

AND

HOW TO KEEP THEM.

CHAPTER I.

INTRODUCTORY.

1. A GREAT many people think that to keep birds is cruel. If it were so, indeed, few would be the cage birds one would wish to see; but happily, on the contrary, for those who, like myself, are fond of the feathered tribe, the more we know about them, the more we are content to think theirs is a happy prison. Not for all birds by any means; some would break their hearts, if they should be kept in cage. The birds of passage, all those that come and go, should never be kept from the sunny skies they seek as the winter comes. We may easily, however, find sufficient pets among our proper house-birds. The Canaries generally, and all the home-bred Finches; plenty of sweet-voiced Linnets; and amongst

1

the foreigners, many tiny creatures, Waxbills, and
Amandavas. When these are safely reared, or once
have been brought to England, we have but to
make them happy ; it would be cruel to expose them
to the misery of being loose, little shivering, trembling
strangers, in an unkindly crowd. Poor little creatures,
if one of them does get out, how fast it flies to seek
some friendly cage ; it knows not the language, the
ways and fashions of the birds around it, nor yet
does it always meet with the kindest welcome from
them. Besides, our home-birds want petting—they
have no wish, so their gay song tells us, to seek a dirty
puddle instead of a crystal bath, to hide from the rain
and cower from the cold, instead of hanging singing in
a pleasant room, conversing now and then with the
friendly company. My Goldfinch, for instance, would
he like, indeed, to go out and breakfast on his own
small means ? Goldie and I greatly take leave to doubt
it ; a flight round the room, while his mistress prepares
the breakfast, is much more to Goldie's mind, and the
moment it is ready, he pops back very briskly into
his cage to eat it. Moreover, would he get such
breakfasts every day alone if he were sent to try ?
And it is said goldfinches are capable of an attachment to hemp seed, that will keep them very regular
in returning at proper hours, even when they are
allowed to go out into the air.

2. But most people forget to reckon on the birds'

social habits; nor do they give them credit for half their loving ways. I have known little pets fly all in a flutter to meet and greet me, when really I thought they would have quite forgotten that they had ever known me; and only let any one nurse a wounded bird, and see if it forgets the benefit received.

3. Besides, they are very clever. I am sure if as many people lived sociably with birds, as with dogs and cats, we should have soon a thousand proofs of their sagacious ways. Speaking for myself, I know quite well by their tones what my birds are wanting, —sometimes it may be only a kindly recognition of a passing friend; but a few days ago when two were fighting and we took no notice, there was little doubt what the conquered wanted,—she called us to her assistance as plainly as if she had spoken.

4. Birds remember, too, even if they are free, those whom they have known. We used at one time to rear many birds, half Canaries and half golden Linnets; and these birds having learnt to sing the canary notes, would be let fly away to build amongst the shrubs. It was a doubtful experiment, so many of them got caught; but it used to be very pleasant while walking amongst the trees to hear a sweet voice calling to us, and to see one of our former charges flying on before us, passing from one tree to another, bowing, and fluttering, and keeping up the talk, as long as we on our part would condescend to answer.

5. I do not know how real Canaries can be best brought to stand our cold English winters. Our own grounds were remarkably warm, and shut in amidst hills, and there were many thick belts of laurels, and dense clumps of evergreens, which certainly afforded a good deal of shelter, so that we had no lack of English birds of all kinds, from the Wrens that built their exquisite round nest in the creepers upon the wall, to the Robin Redbreasts in their greenhouse home; the Goldfinches in the larches, the Thrushes in the laurels, and the gold-crested Wrens on an apple branch. Alas, for the cherry-trees, there were nests in them; but when seven Nightingales would be heard on a summer's evening, singing upon the lawn, we felt well repaid for any little damage that their race might do us. And thus it was, that I began to study birds, picking up those half-fledged little ones that tumbled from the nests, making daily rounds amongst those we knew, and at last, where we felt well acquainted, (as amongst those who built each year in the same place regularly), becoming very daring, we went carrying with us teacups of bread and water, and kindly volunteered our help to the old birds in their ménage. I never knew a nest deserted for us, the old birds would sit on a tree next door, and watch with much benignity while all the little things would stretch out their heads and open their mouths at once,

thinking themselves very lucky because they all got fed. Living thus amongst them, it was natural by degrees to get into a birdish way of viewing things; feeling the chief consideration to be not what might answer, but what was really natural: and though it is indisputable that in a cage, the state of birds is so far unnatural that they are deprived to a great degree of exercise, still they are in very frequent motion; and in a room or aviary, no one who watches them for a single day, can think they are too stationary.

CHAPTER II.

BIRDS TO KEEP.

1. THE heading, Birds to Keep, gives a wide range, indeed. So various are the tastes, so numerous the birds, so different the accommodation in different persons' reach. But to speak only of taste. There are the many who delight in a talking bird—a Starling or a Jackdaw, or perhaps a Magpie—and when the accomplished bird has come, as these birds do, to some untimely end, the wicker cage is filled by, perhaps, a Thrush or Blackbird; for I do not observe that pets of the Jackdaw genus are frequently replaced.

Then there are the pretty white Doves; they are

general favourites for the outside of windows; but none of these are exactly room birds, they require to be out of doors so much, and in such airy quarters.

2. We have, however, song birds enough, amongst which to choose; and though, I think, generally, each person is fond of one kind particularly, yet even thus the many " Warblers " (as the soft-billed tribes are called), and the numerous hardy English or Canary-finches, give scope for choice to those who do not wish to keep up a foreign aviary. Of the Finch class, and those immediately resembling it, we have a goodly number; the many kinds of each, too, differing widely in their song and plumage, as, for example, the Green Canary—a little sober, greenish brownly dressed bird, and the brilliant Jonquille, with his jet-black tuft.

There are Goldfinches with their tricks and Bull-finches with their tunes, the sweet-voiced Linnets of many sorts and colours, Chaffinches, more rarely met with, at least in English aviaries, than they deserve to be, and the pretty, black-headed Aberdevines or Siskins, which pair with the Canaries.

3. The soft-billed birds, or Sylvia, are almost still more numerous; their very names are tempting, and one longs to have a room of " Warblers," including the universal favourites, the Woodlark and the Night-ingale. There is, however, a wide starting-point from which tastes may diverge. Some, for instance, delight

in concerts of Nightingales on the lawn, or heard in the depth of woods in quiet evening drives, but in rooms they fancy that they are rather loud. Wood-larks, on the contrary, with their *trills* of music, are almost too sad to listen to, except in a garden aviary, where they may be happy.

4. For garden aviaries, Warblers are perfect; they need much care and to be enclosed in winter; but to a large conservatory, a little greenhouse full of shrubs and warblers, or even large cages, half hidden among the orange-trees and camellias, would be a charming adjunct. There. protected from cold and provided against starvation, the birds would be happy, and their songs would be songs of joy; in rooms, shut up in little cages, they fret out their hearts, and if they sing it is the low sweet melancholy note which laments for their own free air.

Still it must be owned that when they have once been caught and have been long confined, much more when they have been brought up from the nest, it is better to let them stay and to make them then as happy as is possible, since they would be very helpless left to their own resources.

5. In the hard-billed class, my own special favourites amongst English birds are the Goldfinches and Linnets, Bullfinches and Robins; they are such sweet-voiced singers, and learn other notes so readily, that even the warblers' songs are not lost to my room

entirely. In this way it is really pleasant to hear those lovely strains, knowing all the time that the sweet little singer is revelling in the intensest happiness of its short bird life, poised on a waving branch, singing in the sunshine, turning and quivering in the ecstasy of its song.

A German yellow Canary I bought last spring, is in voice the sweetest of Woodlarks; and as in disposition it is the vainest and most affectionate of Canary birds, it is delightful to see its happiness and to hear its song when it sits bending down, fairly singing at one.

6. The warbler tribe, as its name implies, includes most of our sweetest songsters; Nightingales and Blackcaps, Robin Redbreasts and Jenny Wrens, White-Throats and Garden Warblers; all these are included, while Larks may be reckoned with them as regards the practical difficulties and objections to their being kept in cages. Neither the Larks, Wrens, nor Robins leave this country, however, in winter, as the others do. For those like the Nightingale, who are birds of passage, it is a great aggravation of their many miseries to be prevented going; and they die in great numbers when the time of migration comes. I say an aggravation—but think of a Lark incaged! There is a quiet remark in Bechstein quoted by most bird-writers, that Woodlarks seldom live more than one year in prison; and that the cause of their death is " commonly a broken leg." This is too suggestive

for keeping Woodlarks happily, and I am glad to say that I have never had one, and cannot describe them, therefore.

7. But for the gold-crest Wrens—loveliest of small birds, our English humming birds; they are happy enough in a latticed bell cage, closely covered in winter with green baize at night, perches wrapped in flannel, and all sorts of luxuries in the way of warmth. They generally sleep away the winter in some wool-lined hole—a warm room or a *plant case* in one is therefore best for them; the glass lined with a fine woollen net, and a large myrtle or a tiny fir-tree for them to hang on like balls of brown and gold. They greatly like a little fresh earth to peck and scratch at; and flies are dainties, for these birds are of the soft-billed race.

Bread and milk, a roll, or some biscuit powder squeezed through boiling water, and beaten up with cold milk is their best food. I fancy egg, too, might suit them; but they *must* have some insects. Ants' eggs particularly they like. Bechstein says that to touch rape or camellia seed is death to them; but I cannot vouch for this from experience.

8. Robins, again, may be made so tame and happy in a room or greenhouse, that it would be a pity to attempt to keep them in a cage. They have to be cultivated in the cold snowy weather, or to be brought up on familiar terms from the nest. I

think it might be allowable to have a nest of young Robins brought up in a cage by the old birds, the tamest of which might be kept for the greenhouse or for hopping about in a poultryhouse, where Robby, being pugnacious, agrees better with cocks and hens than with birds of his own size: a pair of Robins will feed with the chickens, take all sorts of liberties, from a ride on the cock's back downwards—and at the earliest glimpse of spring will build in the same enclosure ; and this plan is much better than bringing Redbreasts into real confinement. The poultry-woman is sure to complain that " the Robins eat all the fowls' meat;" but that I think will be the gravest difficulty that will be met with here.

9. Robins are much the hardiest of their class. The soft-billed birds more generally require keeping in winter in a well-warmed room ; and even then there are difficulties arising from smoke or dust.

10. To proceed to the hard-billed class. In my own opinion no birds equal Goldfinches and Canaries for varieties of song, affectionate ways and prettiness. Linnets are such frightful gluttons that if they are kept in an aviary well supplied with a variety of food, either they will become perfect balls of fat and die of over-eating, or else the other birds must be almost deprived of hemp seed. They are, however, very amusing birds; and I always maintain that there is a great deal of character in their faces. They are

also easily tamed and very funny in their naughty doings, poking in their heads wherever they are not wanted, while no one need dwell on the sweetness of their note. They are clean birds, and much enjoy a good bath. I have a cage with five Linnets and a Chaffinch, which afford me much amusement, and they agree very well together.

11. The Chaffinch, in an aviary, seems generally looked down upon; and yet, I can see no reason why this should be, or for the expression, "only a common chaffinch." In Germany and France these lively, active birds are extremely popular; and in England it seems to me that only those who have never tried them, continue to despise them.

They are very clean birds, always pluming and pruning themselves, and their sharp call as they hop about, is very sweet, though shrill. Their song in England is not much thought of, but Bechstein preferred them to all other cage birds, and I should certainly recommend them as an addition to any aviary. For a single bird, too, a Chaffinch is easily managed, and is a very affectionate, clever little fellow. Square cages in this case are a good deal used for them, but they like best to have a good space to hop along. However, for single cages I know not whether Goldfinches, Chaffinches or Bullfinches, really are the nicest.

12. Bullfinches are very nice birds to have, they

are extremely dandified, which is always an advantage, as it keeps them employed; and they are not generally very rapacious birds, though their habit of pecking off buds, probably in the hope of an insect inside, has apparently gained them a character of being so. There are hardly any birds that may be made more tame than these; and the delight with which they puff out their feathers, and sidle, and bow, and stand up tall when spoken to, is something charming, too amusing almost sometimes; one wastes so much time talking to them.

13. Goldfinches, too, are great pets; it may well be said, "if they were foreign birds, how popular they would be." To make them very tame, they should be brought up from the nest by being fed through a quill, or tended in a cage by the old birds, till fledged, as I shall explain hereafter; and this is the best and happiest as well as the most certain plan, as the birds cannot miss so much the liberty that they have never known. Still birds taken in very snowy weather often get so happy, and seem so thoroughly at home, that in their cases, any idea of cruelty in keeping them is removed entirely.

14. In concluding this chapter, it may be as well to say, that birds do not tame so quickly when liable to be frightened: any sudden noises seem to jar their nerves, and to render them more shy. It is a very bad plan, therefore, to take all our friends

to see our last new pet, and will greatly delay or prevent it from becoming tame.

The first day or two in a new abode is of itself quite enough to upset so small a head, and the quieter it is in all ways, and the fewer faces it sees, and voices it hears, the better it will get on. These cautions sound almost too minute; but people are apt to be exuberant in their kindly intended pettings of a new arrival.

CHAPTER III.

ON TAMING BIRDS.

1. EVERY one seems to fancy that in taming birds there is some peculiar art, some secret means by which the object can be attained directly.

Even if this were the case, I doubt if the secret would be very greatly valued; but it would aggravate me dreadfully if anybody else could get my birds to be at once on the same friendly footing as that on which we live together.

In point of fact, birds are very exclusive in the choice of their special friends; it takes a long time of kind words and petting, to make the little creature perfectly at its ease, and to attach it to one, which is really *taming*. It is extremely easy, for instance, to get a bird to take a seed or fruit when offered it, after a day's acquaintance ; but to have it talk to us, and flutter towards us, and hop about upon us, and try for a game of play, is a great deal more agreeable ; and I had rather see my birds tug at my lace or ribbon, and dash away and come back again by another road, looking very naughty, than have any amount of tameness shown by accepting hempseeds.

Knowing that how to tame birds is a question of so much interest to all who keep them, perhaps I may venture to write about my own pets more than I would do otherwise, in the hope that the description of some of their ways and of how they have been managed may bring the same pleasant interest into the easy reach of many other persons. In the summer, when it can be managed easily, the birds without doubt do better out of doors protected by a shady tree during the day, and some water-proof kind of curtain at night, and during rain ; while if in a room, the more the windows can be kept open the better they will thrive. It is chiefly in winter, therefore, and in early spring that I have them generally flying about my room. For an hour or two daily, it is a great amusement to all parties concerned ; their number being from two or three to about a dozen ; for it is difficult to study the characteristics, and have special acquaintance with the personal peculiarities of a much larger tribe.

2. When young birds are brought up from the nest, either reared in a cage by the old birds, or by hand feeding, they are naturally quite tame; but there is often much difficulty in obtaining them, and when they are caught just fledged, as is usually the case with those offered for sale in the early summer in London, and other towns, it is exceedingly difficult to accustom them to their food; and, with a beginner, certainly, if not on a remarkably good system, nine-tenths of the birds so bought will die in the first week. The best way possible, is to find a good-natured old bird, though that is a mere chance; still in a good stock of birds it does often happen that one will respond to the poor little birds' entreaties to be fed and comforted. The young Goldfinches especially are very tender, but charming if they will live. The rearing of young birds, however, is described in another chapter; my business now is chiefly about the taming.

3. Birds that are caught in winter, often take to the cage more kindly than would be expected; and, indeed, in London I do not think it is of much use to let them loose again under the supposition that they are unhappy. The chances are that they would die at that cold season, either of cold or hunger, or that they would fall again into the bird-catcher's hands.

4. Many birds are so wild at first in a change of

place, that it is impossible to know whether any are really newly caught. At any rate, where it is feared that such is the case, the cage should be put into a quiet place shaded with a green woollen cover, so that the inmate may not see persons moving about the rooms, and it should be supplied with abundance of whatever is supposed to be its favourite food. Hemp seeds generally fulfil this requirement. It is an immense advantage to have a large cage made like the " trap " or " store " cages, in which German canaries are generally sold. The wooden bars do not hurt a bird like any made of wire, and these cages are also warmer, and probably feel to the birds more of a protection. I recommend, therefore, a cage for new-comers, made like four traps in one.

Whatever the cage may be, the food and the shading are essential points ; and the bird, if it does not see where a voice comes from, will often get very soon familiar with the tone of its mistress's, even before the cage begins to be kept uncovered, and when the seed is given it will be getting accustomed to the voice that talks to it. After the first day or two, I do not leave the seed tin always in the cage, but take it away after each meal for a little while, taking the opportunity of having a talk with the bird when I give it back, and gradually bringing the cage nearer to me as it gets more tame. The water, of course, is always in the cage, and this must not be understood to imply a starving system; I do not think making a bird hungry and miserable—which in bird-language are synonymous—would be likely to make it quickly become at home; the seed is, at any rate, never kept long away; my only object is to obtain the chance of talking to the bird and making friends with it while it is partly engaged in eating. A single bird in a cage tames very much more quickly than when there are two or three. If, as spring comes (for I am supposing newly-caught birds to be bought in the winter only), the birds do not seem to have become quite happy, I think that it would be then much better to give them back their liberty: still, as far as my experience goes, I do not think this sacrifice will be often called for, they attach themselves so soon to their companions as well as to their owners.

5. I speak of birds bought in the autumn and winter only, because it seems cruel to think of buying old birds at any other season, excepting those which (like foreign birds and Canaries) are always kept indoors. The bird-catchers frequently obtain them by making their own nest the trap which catches them; and when one thinks of the little diamond eyes shining out upon us with such apparent fearlessness, though all the while we see how the poor heart is beating, it does seem very cruel to remove the faithful mother from the pretty nest of which she is so fond.

6. The rules for bird-taming are very few—or rather there are few that are really general, the application of them varying with almost every bird. I think one secret is always to respond to all the bird's advances ; if it asks for a seed, to give it one ; and if it pecks at your fingers, to produce the same reward ; and in the especial treats, too, it is a great matter always to give them yourself, and separately ; the birds do not understand finding them in the cage, or having them sent to them; on the other hand, they learn quickly to associate all their pleasures with their mistress who prepares them.

7. Winning a bird's heart is very amusing work, and if it does seem at first a little like " cupboard love," yet, after all, how, but by our actions, can they understand our kind feelings towards them ?   And I will say that their hearts once gained, their attachment is faithful and quite disinterested.

My little Bullfinch, for instance. Poor little Bullie, with her brown satin dress, and her velvet head-dress, she does sing *such* a song. It is very low and extremely long, I wish I could add musical, but that is certainly not its most striking feature. Still, Bullie is an affectionate little bird, and if her song is very droll and small, we cannot find fault with anything, while she is so evidently doing her best to please us, leaving her seed at any time for the pleasure of talking to us. Very tame, too, is she, not to say familiar; solitude is her greatest grievance, and she is heard complaining loudly, if ever for a moment she is condemned to her own society.*

8. My present especial room stock consists of three Goldfinches, eight Canaries, and one Bullfinch; and while I write these words, nine small birds are hopping all about. In fact, when the cage doors open, they generally all fly down in a whirl upon me. I turn my head, and three are perched, conversing sociably upon my pillow; and as I resume my sentence, one that has just washed, flies briskly across the room, perches upon my head, and with a tremendous shake commences the arrangement of his very disordered toilette.

The various characters are a great amusement, as they are cautious, polite, presumptuous or condescending. Charlie, for instance (all my birds have names), comes, when spoken to, to the edge of his cage, and looking down superior from his height upon me, vouchsafes to warble me a song in the lowest and sweetest of all sweet Woodlark tones.

And then there is Tuck, he is a very rapacious

---

* Very melancholy is the sequel of this Bullfinch's history. Some time after the foregoing passage was written, Bullie was unavoidably banished for a while from her mistress's room. Every one thought she would have been happy in the society of other birds, but no; for the first day or two she cried very much, and then she refused to eat, and died within a week. No one had any idea that the poor bird was pining, and it was a real trouble to lose so warm-hearted a pet.

Goldfinch, and in all ways, impetuous. Now the other morning Tuck's seed ran short; at least he had none left but rape, of which he makes but small account, and I could not think what ailed the little bird, he shrieked so meaningly, and stared at me so hard. At last it got quite alarming, and I rang to have Tuck's cage brought near; and then the way in which my friend sidled along to his empty seed-box, and put in his head and pulled his beak out empty, looking me hard in the face and screaming with anger all the time; it was quite a farce, and Tuck had to accept many a word of ignominy before he got his breakfast. I hope these instances will be enough to show that my plan of taming, simple though it is, has hitherto answered well. The birds I have now have none of them been in my possession much more than a year; and except in cases where some (such as various kinds of Linnets, Chaffinches, &c.,) have been sent up to me from distant parts of the country, they are all London bought. However, I think my readers will allow that my birds are quite as familiar as they need be, though I do not fancy many of them have had the advantage of being brought up from the nest.

9. A very great point in such cases is never to be the means of really *frightening* the birds at all; in letting them go into a cage, for instance, to put the doors together so as for them to walk in themselves;

to avoid startling them by sudden movements, or by
snapping the seed-boxes round, and hooking the
doors with a jar, and always to talk to them and
coax them while performing any alarming offices.

I think it a particularly good plan, at any rate at
first, to have two cages similarly fitted up, and to
have one each morning entirely prepared for the
bird's reception, the seed for the day, and the water
ready, the floor well sanded, and even the green
food put in, so that when the doors of the two are
opened the inmates can just hop comfortably into
their freshly prepared breakfast room : it saves a
great deal of time and fluttering, if the birds are new;
and is an amusing scene, if they are impatiently
watching for the doors to open.

10. This plan of course involves the slight expense
of an extra cage, but I think its effect is so good on
the bird's health and comfort, that, where several are
kept, it is well worth adopting.

The cages get thus a chance of being thoroughly
cleaned and aired, as they should invariably be prepared for use one morning, all but putting in seed
and water, and then be placed where they will get
plenty of air to freshen them, but without getting
damp, till they are used next day. As far as the birds
are concerned, twice a-week is sufficient for giving
this thorough cleaning, except in the heat of summer :
but if the cages are kept in a sitting-room, every-day

is not at all too often to keep them really nice, and nothing conduces more to a bird's own health, and to the unruffled beauty of its plumage, than this attention. The chief advantage, however, which makes me advise it here, is the entire avoidance of everything alarming. A strange hand coming near the cage may be rather startling; and it is seldom that the birds are entirely fed and cared for by their own mistress, to whom they are more accustomed. To give admission merely into a nice fresh cage all ready prepared for breakfast, is, however, an office most ladies would rather like.

11. Perhaps the most amusing plan, as the birds grow tame, is that which I alluded to in my Goldfinch's case—to let the birds out for a short, brisk flight while their cage is put ready; and if an aviary cage is used, which cannot be changed each day or two, this plan is most convenient, as well as very pleasant. My own room at these times presents a droll scene; as the birds being let out just at breakfast time, all their attention is instantly directed to assisting at mine; and though there is a sort of understanding about not coming on the cloth, birds are apt to evade it by a sudden spring; and I remember one morning three little culprits, one at the edge of my breakfast-cup, another making dashes against the loaf, and a third sipping, in a methodical manner, some syrup from my plate.

It may be considered a peculiar advantage in the taming of my present stock, that a long illness has kept me much in their society, so that they have had ample time to become accustomed to me. I do not, however, think myself that others will find any extra difficulty from the want of this privilege. Birds I had as a child were, if possible, still more tame, though, being kept in a little room where I learned my lessons, they certainly did not enjoy too much of my society. On my side there has been the advantage of ample time in which to observe their ways and to learn their language, far more intelligible than any one could suppose. Such radiantly happy things they are, sitting on picture-frames all round the room, actually shouting in their joyous songs, and then chasing each other round, singing and flying, the conqueror pouring out such triumphant music!

CHAPTER IV.

BIRDS IN A SITTING-ROOM.

1. THERE are few things more popular in all sorts of rooms than a bird-cage—perhaps with a single inmate, perhaps with a pair of birds, or perhaps with even a whole long line of the lovely Amandavas or the pretty Waxbills; and the expensive bird, who

pipes three tunes, is possibly less beloved and treasured than the poor brown Linnet or the smoky Bullfinch, whose song is called music only by a partial mistress.

It would be, I think, a great deal more pleasant to help such single bird-owners to manage their pets well, than to give instructions how to arrange an aviary of three hundred, which seems always to me so utterly uninteresting. One bird, or even a few dozen, may be known and be made friends of, but this it is evident that three hundred cannot be.

However, I must only say that this chapter will be devoted to birds kept in cages—in the usual small sort of cages, that is; thus, whether the stock consists of one or twenty, it need make no difference in the advice for each.

2. First, as to choice. I have already said that Bullfinches, Goldfinches, Canaries or Chaffinches are what seem to me most fitted to live alone. If a pair are kept, they should be Canaries, Goldfinches, or the Java Sparrows. Bullfinches are not so interesting when there are two in a cage together; and Chaffinches, I fear, are rather disposed to fight, and constantly beat their wives.

Even Goldfinches sometimes " swear" considerably; the others, on the contrary, are pleased to be together, and live all the year round on the most friendly terms. The English Wrens, and all the little foreign birds, Waxbills, &c., who live in large parties all in one cage, are also extremely interesting. They are not a very expensive tribe, and, excepting care as to warmth, do not seem to be difficult to manage well. They look very pretty sitting all of a row on the perch, singing in a soft, low voice by turns, spreading out their fan-tails, in a wonderfully quick manner, and sometimes skirmishing when bed-time comes, not to be outside.

3. These pretty little foreigners, and also our own Wrens, should always have thick green baize curtains to cover their cage at night; and if they are left in a sitting-room the housemaid should be desired, on no account, to uncover the cage on a winter's morning. A far safer plan is to let the cage be carried each evening into a warm, comfortable room, to remain there for the night. Everybody knows the anecdote of Mr. Herbert's little gold-crested Wrens, who used to sleep at night under the sofa cushions, but being taken out one morning before the drawing-room had got thoroughly well warmed were all dead in a very few hours after.

In keeping birds there are many ways of adding to their happiness; and to all such pets a bright gleam of sunshine, for instance, on a fine spring or even winter's day, may be made a great enjoyment, if the cage is placed in it. The little things seem so much to like it, and puff out their feathers, and dress themselves so busily; and then I always fancy that they like to see flowers; and we are not the losers if this is indeed the case, for neither birds or flowers ever look half so pretty as when they are mixed together. I may mention here that many of my own smaller cages are often hung in a plant case.

Cold is one of the greatest dangers cage-birds have to be guarded from. In an aviary there are more birds together, who keep one another warm, and they are not necessarily so near to the wires, which are said to absorb a great deal of heat.

Besides giving them every chance of a little sunshine, they should be protected carefully from the draught of open windows; even in the summer time the cage should never stand directly in a draught. Hot sunshine is another extreme to avoid. People are apt to leave a room with the sun just coming on a cage, and to forget that long before they return it will shine with all its force on the poor little bird.

4. Frights of any sort are also to be avoided. Lightning and thunder often kill delicate birds, especially if the blinds are up, and if they are left alone. It is always safer during storms to cover up the cages, especially when the latter are of an open kind.

5. When cages are kept in a room it is best to make a point of each being cleaned out daily, if the

cage itself is not changed, as I have elsewhere advised. If a bird is at that time allowed to stretch its wings in a flight, it will always go back fast enough to its breakfast: if it were, on the contrary, to be let out in the evening, it is ten to one but that it would perch on the top of its own cage, outside, and refuse decidedly to go to bed at all.

6. Then arises the unpleasant necessity of catching Dickie, an operation which all birds do especially detest; and I hardly like it better than they do themselves; for it is nervous work to grasp such a fragile creature. Very funny it feels, however, when matters are reversed, and they claw you, sitting upright on one finger, and taking such tight hold if you give them a little ride; and when they are caught they peck so very hard. Sometimes birds scream out when they are caught as if they were half killed; at first I thought they were, and was alarmed accordingly; but it seems in reality that these were old hands, who had been used to be caught before under rather rougher handling, and thus very prudently they cried out in good time; however, the moment I presented and they accepted a huge lump of biscuit, both parties became consoled, and we had no more shrieks.

7. When birds are kept in these small single cages, they ought to have less hemp or rape seed than if they have more exercise. Canary seed,

crumbs of stale bread, or of perfectly plain biscuits, water-cress and groundsel, should be their staple food—only Bullfinches do better with a good deal of rape—and Canaries, generally, require a little more hemp. In small cages, or open seed-boxes, the hemp should never be mixed with the other seed, as the bird will plunge in his head and dash out all the rest in search of it.

8. The coarse river sand impregnated with iron, as shown by its reddish tinge, is a great preserver of most birds' health, as they swallow a good deal of it, as well as enjoy walking and scraping in it.

A rusty nail in the water glass, or a thread of saffron, is very often useful ; it is especially so in the autumn during the time of moulting, when greater warmth and greater quiet, as well as more nourishing food, are proper for the bird, which may be considered an invalid. The food should also be softer, hemp seeds being bruised ; and plenty of green food should be given, with some plantain,—commonly called rat's tails. A hard-boiled egg chopped up is very good, when the bird seems to eat but little ; if his appetite is good, there is not much cause to be uneasy for him : often, indeed, birds do little but eat and sleep while moulting, at which time they do not sing. A few insects or ants' eggs, if they can be obtained (as they can be in London), are particularly welcome to most kinds of birds.

9. Very pleasant it is in a room if a special pair of pets begin to make a nest. At the moment I write this, one pair of Canaries, within a yard of my head, are thus engaged, and very amusing it is to watch them. The right thing for their building is a cage about twenty-two inches by sixteen, in which there are two small square compartments, intended to hold seed-boxes. I always think it best to remove these boxes, and then filling the space with small sprays of fir or box, the nest is made to fit in in a pretty way. If the sprays are cut in February the fir generally does not lose its leaves. These nest rooms have small round holes for doors, and the bag of wool and hair should be tied securely outside the cage to the wire bars.

10. The instinct and cleverness of birds is really very wonderful, when one has time to watch them. This very pair, for instance :—it is the cock bird's duty to feed the hen while sitting, and the gentleman here being young and apparently rather giddy, his wife evidently considered that he required training before the time arrived for his duties to commence. And a very funny affair between the two they made of it ; for first Mrs. Tuft got into the nest and waited, and then she went down and undutifully pecked her husband without the least explanation ; at which, Tuft, who is rather timid, looked both alarmed and anxious. Flying back to her nest and seating herself, she again called

Tuft repeatedly, on which Tuft flew up (without any seed) and stood on the door ledge looking more perplexed than ever. I was wondering greatly what she would do with such a weak-minded although willing slave, when I saw her dart from her nest, take Tuft down with her indignantly to the seed tin, in some way evidently indicating his duty, for she had hardly time to fly back and settle herself again in due form upon her nest, before Mr. Tuft arrived with a splendid hemp seed, which, standing on the door ledge, he presented to his lady in the most proper manner.*

11. Birds vary very much as to their talents. The pair I was just speaking of have been peculiarly full of clever tricks; the very first day after Tuft entered the house (Tuft is a beautiful crested Canary, who has only been here a few months) the lady who is now his wife

---

* The evident *plan* of all this did seem to me so astonishing that I was quite delighted when I found, long after this page was written, the following corroboration.—"The male of a Canary bird, which was sitting on her eggs, was more intent on serenading than on feeding her. When this was the case, she would quit her nest and chase him round and round the cage, pecking him violently with her beak, and showing her anger in a variety of ways. She would then return to her nest without attempting to feed herself, and the male would then, like a meek, obedient husband, immediately attend to her wants, carrying her a plentiful supply of seed, groundsel, and egg. He then resumed his song, and she resumed her discipline whenever his notes were too much prolonged."—Jesse's *Gleanings.*

applied herself to his training. I saw her, after carefully letting herself out of her cage in her usual
manner, by turning round the seed-box and then
squeezing through the turnstile thus formed, go
deliberately back and put Master Tuft up to the same
piece of misdirected talent. And then she introduced
him to her favourite dish of crocuses (which was also
mine), and within a very few days she had so perfected
his education, that when I put her into a more
impracticable sort of cage as the most mischievous
bird I had, I was forced to put Tuft into prison also,
as he was found to have become a perfect master of
all her naughty tricks.

I will add hereafter a list of birds suited for single
cages; and mention also the kind of cages best for
each to have.

CHAPTER V.

VARIOUS SPECIAL BIRDS.

1. THERE are very few people who have not at some
time or other possessed a Canary. They are amongst
the easiest of all tame birds to manage; and although
I do not think they possess the very attractive qualities of Goldfinches and Bullfinches, they are still
perhaps the most universally known of all the cage

birds. Their food cannot be better than one part hemp seed to three parts of canary; groundsel, chickweed, or watercress being made a daily food, rather than an occasional dainty, as it too often is, to the bird's great injury.

The price of Canaries is very moderate; a very good bird may be got for five shillings, and hens are not generally more than two shillings. In buying them, the birds which seem moderately shy, are generally the best; an inexperienced person is too apt to be attracted by a very quiet manner; they seem so tame that they are bought quite eagerly, but unhappily they are apt to die soon after: the too great quietness being often caused by illness.

A real good bird will make no end of a fuss; pretending to be a vast deal shyer than it really is, hopping from perch to perch, twisting its head about, and having, in fact, an infinity of pretty airs and graces!

Bird dealers, again, always recommend the birds which sing *loudly;* and this to many is not at all desirable; the lower the tone the prettier and sweeter many would think the song.

An immense advantage in favour of Canaries is, that they build so readily in cages. I do not know anything more pretty than the little brood just leaving the nest, the flutter of the old birds, and their tremendous pride; many a time my birds have fairly called me to see. They have a peculiar clear note which always means they want something, and on the days when the brood were just commencing to hop, it was quite impossible for the proud mamma to let anybody pass her door without giving information of what was to be seen.

One successful bird-fancier told me that he had kept as many as four-and-twenty Canaries loose in an aviary about eight feet square, of which only six were cocks ; so that in fact he was making it just like a poultry yard. But this is a plan I do not like at all. The poor mother birds get so dreadfully overworked, and besides, it is impossible they should be half so happy.

Mrs. Tuft, for instance, has laid her first egg to-day, and is in a state of the profoundest bliss. Mr. Tuft, having looked in once or twice by candle-light to see that all's right upstairs, is now seated on his perch close by, warbling the very sweetest of all sweet-whispered songs ; but if Tuft had three other wives and families claiming his attention, how could he manage to do all this ? It is a consolation to me to know that under the Turkish system, from deficiency in attendance, family jars, and unavoidable jealousies, it is extremely seldom that more young birds grow up than would most likely do so if they were let pair comfortably. Of those that are hatched, many die quite young. The hope of gaining a great many young birds would be of course the only object in treating them in this way, for pleasure certainly there would not be in it; but I strongly advise those who want quickly to stock their aviary, to be contented with what some few pairs will do. It is enough too: a single pair will often build four times in a summer, laying four or five eggs each time, and sitting for thirteen days.

Prize birds there are, too, for very ambitious people, and none of these I think are much prettier than the crested, bright Jonque birds (the colour of a jonquille), with full black tufts looking like black wigs.

To gain a prize, however, a great deal of care is necessary, and the rules vary so often that there is hardly time to keep up with their rapid changes. There are Belgians (the present ugly fashion), Lizards, Jonques, mealy (yellow and white), and the fancy kinds, all amongst prize birds. Some Canaries have red eyes; but this gives a look of weakness, and they are very delicate.

The wild Canary is of a very dark greenish brown hue, almost as dark as an English Linnet, and excessively graceful and pretty in its movements.

For birds merely to keep, however, the very nicest I think are the beautiful little German birds, of which quantities come over every year about Christmas. This breed is rather delicate and exquisitely pretty, small, neatly made, quiet, graceful things, with very sweet voices generally, and I can answer for their becoming quite familiar. The crested birds are the cleverest, I think, and they are very tame. Hopping up to one's hand, and pecking it, just to suggest how acceptable a little bread would be, and, fighting like Turks, pecking and screaming; beating their wings, and scratching away with their fine sharp claws if one chances to interfere with the arrangements, and to incur the sovereign displeasure of their funny little majesties.

Canaries are, moreover, very healthy birds, and live a long time in cages. I was consulted the other day about a bird supposed to be fifteen years old. Canaries are easily kept,—eating most kinds of seed, —though hemp and canary are the most proper food for them. During the laying and nesting season, they should also have some maw seed, and a little bread and milk, always freshly mixed.

When they are allowed to fly about in a room, they will spend whole hours alternately bathing and crawling along the window ledge to dry their feathers on the wood which the sun has warmed. And there they often sit all day, pluming themselves, and basking, and shaking out their dresses.

2. Few birds are more popular than the handsomely attired and affectionate-natured Bullfinch. Its shape, indeed, is against it,—being of a rather heavy make, which sometimes causes its movements to be more

amusing than graceful. Its own note, too, I confess,
is not of the most musical. Still, putting aside the
sweetness of its acquired song, I hardly know any
bird I had not sooner miss than Bully, there is something so taking in its engaging ways.

The Bullfinch seems to be also one of the few
birds which may be brought indoors when old, and
made really happy, more as a visitor than as a
prisoner. If the old birds are caught in the winter
time when they are wanting food, they will very
quickly become extremely tame; and then, when
spring returns, they may often be trained to come and
go in and out of the house, and to hop about their
mistress on the lawn, ruffling up their feathers, and
talking and sidling in a most taking manner. Even
should one be allowed to build out of doors, the
intimacy need not cease, as a Bullfinch has been
often known to return after a short absence, bringing
with her a fine young brood to be introduced to their
mamma's old friends. At the same time these birds
seem perfectly at home when kept entirely indoors, and
are well contented as long as they have company.

When one wants to train a bird to be an accomplished singer, it is a great point to remove it when
extremely young from the nest, before it acquires any
of the old bird's notes. The food in this case should
be of bread on which boiling water has been poured
and pressed off, milk being then added and a little

oatmeal. This should be given at the end of a quill with a notch cut in it a little distance up; the food must be given very often, from sunrise to sunset, and the nestlings must be between whiles warmly covered up.

Hemp seed shelled and pounded up with bread is one of the best of foods; and hard-boiled egg chopped up altogether, and mixed with grated bread. The latter, perhaps, is that which answers most universally for birds taken young from nests. They must be kept also excessively clean; the best plan is a cage with some moss in it or bran, and a piece of flannel that can be replaced daily. Under the flannel the more feathers there are the better.

In learning to sing, a Bullfinch is best kept quite alone, and everything should be done to make his lessons pleasant. Whistling a tune repeatedly is the way that answers best; but a tune slowly played is by degrees picked up, if the little pupil has at all a good ear for music.

3. There may be sometimes a little doubt about keeping Goldfinches, as they are certainly natives of the English woods; and yet I always console myself by observing what extremely happy birds they are under favourable circumstances even in what we call their prison. If loose in the room, they very seldom sit upon the window frame, or seem to look out longingly, and when they have got out there

is no bird I have known so often return to the cage.

These birds are certainly most elegant little creatures, and I should be afraid to say how many hours daily they would appear quite happy in a minute attendance to their toilette duties; they are also some of the most affectionate as well as the liveliest and prettiest of all the birds I know, and their great charm is, that like Bullfinches they are personal in their devotion; they will be on the most familiar terms with their own mistress, hopping about on her hand, peeping between her fingers, and nibbling at her pen; and yet if another person enters, darting up to the curtain pole, or perching on a picture frame, and by no means affable.

It is rather rare that a pair of Goldfinches should build in confinement;—the best chance for their doing so is when they are flying about a room fitted up with a sort of thick hedge of pine branches cut in February so as to keep their leaves, or with a thick bush or two of gorse fastened securely in one corner of the room at a good height from the floor.

I own I suspect that some of my Goldfinches once were wild; but if so they have not much to complain of now, for they look very happy in their russet dress, shading down to white, and their black feathers with the clear white spangles and brilliant crimson heads. There they sit on the top of the fir-tree

pluming themselves, and twittering, and playing all
sorts of tricks.

Goldfinches to become accomplished should always
be brought up from the nest. But though they
are certainly more difficult to tame when they are
old, the little " grey pates," *i.e.* birds of the same
season, are most difficult to rear, unless they
can be brought up by old birds from the nest. If
reared like Bullfinches, adding a little strong tea in
one of the water glasses, when they begin to moult,
saves the lives of many of them.

In any place where birds are kept at all, I think
that a tolerable number of these pretty Goldfinches are
really irresistible. I do not believe that they hurt
one another much, even though they do pretend to
quarrel, in spite of their long sharp bills and their
tremendous clamour, which sounds so very warlike;
and they look so ridiculous when they take offence,
and sit sulky on their perch, holding it extremely
tight all the time, sitting almost on their feet, but
at the same time so upright as to seem not unlikely
to tumble over backwards.

A fir-tree in a pot in a sitting-room, and three
or four Goldfinches to hop about upon it, is as
constant an amusement as anything of the sort I
know; and they are wonderful birds, too, for retiring
to their cage. After an hour or two's play, and a
good bath, if attainable, they hop off home again,

and perch themselves in their proper cage with the most solemn dignity. One of my birds was out one day while the places of the furniture were being altered, and he was hardly put to it where to go for safety; but his own cage was there, and though it was on the stand at that moment being moved, in flew my friend, and there he sat the whole time.

4. If we wish to tame a Robin, one of the most pleasant of home pets, it must be done very gradually, making great friends with a young bird and feeding it, when it will often come contentedly to roost in-doors in the colder weather, and will cheerfully intro-duce its small brown brood to hop about before us later in the season on the gravel walk. And one tame Robin will often bring in another, when they are at peace, which is very rare, though I have several which seem very happy. A young bird brought up from a nest is a most agreeable pet; he ought in that case to possess a cage, but to be allowed to go in and out at will. My own favourite little bird hops about my room continually, and the instant I call either him or any one else, he comes hopping up with great long hops, to answer to his name or see what is going on.

He eats egg and bread crumbs, German paste, hemp and canary seeds, and must have abundant water. Yesterday I had my windows open, and Bobby was kept in his cage all the morning; so towards evening we shut the windows and let the poor Robin out, shortly after which he was found drenched in a watering pot, which was standing near my plant-stand with a little water only (very luckily as it happened,) remaining at the bottom. He had certainly not been out ten minutes before he had discovered it, and enjoyed his bath.

I find it very difficult to decide what bird is nicest. Bobby certainly is an uncommon favourite, one never speaks to him without such an instant answer, and he sings so sweetly. It would be, however, a real grief to me, if writing thus of my Robin led any one to attempt catching old birds to keep ; where one might be happy, I am certain, a thousand would be miserable, and I should feel a traitor to the whole race of Robins. If they are kept, let them be taken from nests, and let them hop about and amuse themselves in a room, and then, I think, they will be quite at home and happy.

CHAPTER VI.

FOOD.

1. THE question of food is often made more trouble-some than it need be, by the idea that the different kinds of birds require different sorts, either of seed or paste. The simplest plan is generally best ; and in

fact, where many birds are together in an aviary, an approximation to the food of each is all that can be attempted.

As a general rule, there is, perhaps, no bird of the hard-billed class which would refuse canary seed, but a few prefer rape ; and while to some a fair share of hemp is necessary, to others it is injurious, as they become too fat.

2. Bechstein gives a most excellent recipe for a universal paste, one on which, he says, thirty or forty birds thrive well in his room, preserving most perfectly the beauty of their plumage. All birds, he says, whatever their natural food, will eat this willingly; and he has had Chaffinches, Goldfinches, Linnets, Siskins (Aberdevines), Robins, Canaries, Larks, Tits, Hedge-warblers, Quails, &c., all feeding on it together. These birds, however, belong chiefly to those which eat only seeds, though a few of them eat insects also, as Larks and the varieties of Tits, which also are largely given to devour green pease and berries. For all these birds it seems well to mix with the paste a little hemp and rape seed ; when the seed can be pounded, the birds certainly like it better, and thus many people devote a coffee-mill entirely to their service.

Of course it is better to let the birds have their own mill ; but should this be inconvenient, as in the case of only one or two, the mill may be perfectly cleansed from both coffee and bird seed, by grinding in it a little stale bread or rice before and after the bird seed is ground ; the seed may also be prepared by pounding. A sort of paste (which I will describe hereafter) is also a good standard food for the warbler class, and for all birds which live on insects and berries, including, that is, Nightingales, Blackcaps, Thrushes, Wrens, Redpoles, &c., with the various Finches and Linnets. For these former birds, however, I always should be inclined, if possible, to omit the milk—at any rate, boiled milk. Mr. Herbert, who seems to have tried many different plans, and to have been one of the most successful managers of these especially delightful songsters, never approved of giving it. The freshly-ground hemp seeds contain, in reality, a milky sort of juice, and a grated carrot also is sufficient to sweeten the mass a little.

Bechstein's authority is certainly very weighty, but it should be remembered that his birds were really *room birds* (Stubenvögel), not cage birds, and that allowance must be made for the constant exercise that this gave scope for, as well as for the greater coldness of the German weather, and throughout his work it is evident that but few of his birds comparatively were kept at all in cages.

3. For the warbler, or soft-billed class, the admixture of dried flies, ants' eggs, or pounded hard-boiled egg, is extremely useful ; and in many instances, the

milk, *when used cold*, will not disagree, though it does when boiled.

Boiled milk is admitted to be unhealthy, raw milk is considered harmless. Therefore, in some instances when cold milk has been found injurious, this may possibly arise from the fact that, though cold, it was not raw, but *scalded* milk. As far as a short trial (with bought milk too) can be depended on, I quite believe the fact is thus accounted for.

4. I proceed to give Bechstein's three recipes, which do not appear to have been since surpassed, as a general food.

Let a supply of wheaten bread be baked without salt—sufficient for three months' use may be done at one time. The loaves should be kept till stale, and then be replaced in the oven when a baking is taken out, and remain there while it cools. The dried bread may then be easily ground or pounded into a kind of meal, which will keep good for three months. A large tea-spoonful of this meal is sufficient for each bird's share, and this should be mixed with three times the quantity of warm milk, *on no account suffered to boil*. This makes a thick paste, which may be chopped up on a board, and is very nourishing.

Poppy seeds or a few flies may with great advantage be mixed up with this paste. Another excellent paste, the one alluded to above as feeding so many birds, is recommended both for its cheapness and its

great simplicity. Soak thoroughly in cold water a
well-baked stale wheaten loaf, press the water out of
it, pour cold milk upon it, and mix it with two-thirds
of its own weight of barley or wheat meal, well ground
and sifted.

A third paste is made thus : Grate a carrot (which
may be kept in sand, in a cool place for a year) on
a grater, which must afterwards be immediately
washed quite clean ; thoroughly soak a penny roll
in cold water, press the water out, and mix the bread
and carrot with two handfuls of wheat or barley meal,
pounding the whole together thoroughly in a mortar.

Except so far as the pounded bread meal itself is
concerned, these pastes must be made entirely fresh
each day ; and the vessels in which they are kept
(Philipps' glass preserve jars answer admirably, with
glass lids) and the feeding trough (of earthenware)
must be very well cleansed each day.

5. The birds do not always take to these pastes
quite kindly. It is often requisite to humour some
dainty individuals by observing their tastes, and
mixing with the paste some of their favourite viands,
poppy seed, pounded hemp, or the universally liked
ants' eggs. Still it cannot be said to give such a
temptation to this and such to another bird, for so
much depends on their up-bringing ; and though
we may know what different ones *ought* to like, it is
by no means sure that they do so.

6. Bechstein records a way of taking ants' eggs, which I think will be found useful, and is no doubt practised in many places in laying up stores for game.

On a fine day in summer the ant-hill is turned over, and the earth containing the eggs being shovelled on to a cloth, a few green boughs are laid on one side, under which immediately the ants convey the eggs. The eggs are then dried in a frying-pan with a little sand, and thus stored away in jars till required for use, when boiling water is poured on them to soften them.

7. The German paste is also a very useful food, particularly for all the soft-billed birds, or warblers. I find it answers best to have this paste made at home, as it is scarcely any trouble. Good materials can then be depended on ; the price is also a third or fourth only of that at which it can be purchased genuine. As far as I know, with the exception of Nightingales, all soft-billed birds will thrive well on this paste, with some grated stale-bread crumbs, and a few canary and hemp seeds now and then as a change. The seeds need not be bruised, as these birds swallow them whole, and are provided with gizzards for their digestion. A few morsels sometimes of quite fresh meat (neither salt meat nor meat that has any salt on it will do), given either raw or cooked, will be good for most of them ; and the Nightingales, in particular, should be chiefly fed on raw meat finely chopped up with some hard-boiled egg. In this

way they will live and sing without insects, though they, as well as Larks, Robins, and other birds of this class, are extremely glad to get any ; and any approach to their most natural food is always a great advantage. A spadeful of mould out of an ants' nest is the greatest treat that such birds can have. My receipt for the German paste is given me by one who seems to be thoroughly acquainted with the ways and tastes of birds, both when wild and when kept in confinement.

Take two tablespoonfuls of melted lard, very free from salt, heat this in a saucepan till it is nearly boiling, add to it four tablespoonfuls of treacle, keeping the saucepan near the fire, but not putting it on again, and stirring the treacle well in gradually. Keeping this mixture still near the fire, but not near enough to do more than keep hot, stir in pea-meal till the whole mass is a stiff, crumbly paste. About three pints and a half of meal go to the above quantity, and a few maw seeds should be finally strewed amongst it.

I give the quantity by measure, thinking it may be the more convenient manner, but the proportions by weight would be two ounces of lard, four of treacle, and three pints and a half of pea-meal. This paste, if kept in one of the glass preserve jars, will be perfectly good for months.

Many bird-keepers in using it grate a piece of very stale bread, and mix the two thoroughly well together.

Most birds are fond of it, and it often tempts a sickly one to eat, while it is an excellent preparation for keeping them in good plumage. German paste, however, should never be bought ready-made at an inferior shop, as many other things are used in it less good for the birds, besides which, damaged pea-meal is continually employed, making the composition extremely unwholesome for them. When this paste is good a well-boiled mealy potato, well beaten up, which is very popular among birds, does also well to mix with it.

The lard in this paste of course supplies a little the place of insects; but there are very few birds which do not seem the better for sometimes having a little food of that kind.

8. Even the Goldfinches, which are supposed to be the strictest vegetarians, will make the completest clearance of anything like greenflies or aphides on a flower stem. When birds are moulting, and especially when they have young broods, some food of this nature seems to be particularly required, and if no insects, such as aphides, or ants' eggs, are forthcoming, some finely chopped hard-boiled egg, or a little chopped-up meat, is a useful substitute for even these hard-billed birds; always being careful that anything of this kind is perfectly fresh and quite untouched by salt. I fully believe myself that all young birds are partly brought up on insects of some description.

9. Watercresses are one of the greatest of all birds' dainties. Groundsel, plantain, chickweed and thistle-seeds for the Goldfinches are also very good. They say, indeed, that in Scotland the " Goldies," or " Goldspinks," are sometimes found half buried in a thistle head. Another grand luxury is a piece of plain biscuit. Few birds will be found to refuse a part of one of Huntley and Palmer's cracknels. I am very particular in what I give my pets; but there is quite an excitement when I open the well-known box, and all call out to beg some. Stuck between the wires, or suspended (by a string through it) from a fir-tree branch, it is very amusing to watch the incessant nibbling till the biscuit is quite finished.

Sugar is not good for singing birds, a little piece of Spanish liquorice in their water glass is much better, and fresh ripe fruit is generally much liked. I think on the whole apples and pears are best; though I do see very black bills in the cherry season, and elderberries also are often much enjoyed.

Lettuce leaves are very good, and may be grown in winter; but young lettuces and Begonias look, unluckily, a good deal alike; and, on the whole, it is preferable that the former should be pulled up. I have not yet forgotten the sudden dab made by Dickie at a special Begonia seedling, which was out of the pot and down her throat before I should have thought she had had time to see it.

10. Unless a very large stock is kept, probably most people will find it least trouble to feed their birds on seed as a general rule. It seems to me the most plain course to take—and my own birds have generally never tasted anything but seed and vegetables, with a little egg, or perhaps a few stale bread-crumbs, for weeks and months together.

There is an exceedingly strong prejudice against giving birds much hemp-seed, it is said to make Bullfinches black, and to turn Goldfinches grey—at least to deprive them of their brilliant plumage.

On this subject I can only mention the caution, and state my own experience, which certainly does not forbid to the Finch tribe generally, especially in the winter, a tolerable allowance of their favourite food. I cannot imagine crimson brighter than my Goldie's head—and all my birds have always had access to a little of it—except young Linnets, which are so gluttonous. Canaries have generally a little allowed to them; but I think it probable that one thing which causes it not to hurt my birds, is that they have always so good a supply of green food, and facilities for bathing, as well as some time for exercise. In the case of both hemp and rape, however, it must be remembered that they are heating foods, containing a large amount of oil.

In the summer, birds having as much green food as they like, often do not eat a very great deal of seed;

but where they are fed entirely upon seed, it would certainly be necessary to make a most marked difference between the summer and winter diet.

Except in the spring with the young, and in the autumn when moulting, the supply of these seeds should therefore a good deal depend on the warmth of the room or aviary, on the amount of exercise, and on the share of green food that can be supplied.

When the birds are exposed to some cold, have exercise and green food, the rape and hemp in the proportion of one to three parts of canary will seldom be found too much. In the summer even, Canaries and other birds in an out-door aviary may generally take this mixture harmlessly, especially when steeped.

11. In buying a new bird, however, it is well to make a point of hearing what its food has been, because, for instance, an old bird brought up without hemp would suffer were it given.

My usual plan has been to have one pound of canary-seed, and to mix with it half-a-pound of rape, the same of hemp, and the same of flax.

The poppy, or maw-seed, I keep separate, and generally give it either mixed with any paste that is used, or strewed on the sand or gravel on the floor of the cage. This red sand is very essential for the health of the birds, and I think these small grains of a popular seed are useful in causing them to scratch about more diligently in it. It should be made an object to get real good seed. Canary should be hard and bright, of a brownish yellow colour, and look white and floury when broken through; it is also very essential, indeed, that it should have been stored where mice cannot get at it. Birds have a horror of seed that mice have been amongst, in fact, they will not eat it unless they are very hungry. Hemp-seed is white inside, and tastes like a nut; rape-seed, which is best, and tolerably new (we used always to have ours sent in from the barn when the wheat was threshed), is round and blackish brown, with a bright yellow kernel looking like yolk of egg. The linseed, or flax, should always be well examined, and that which has a dull and dirty appearance should be avoided, as well as that which, as is often the case, seems stuck together.

Oats are seed for some birds, and groats for some—millet also is a constant food of almost all the little foreigners; but it is not necessary to speak of these things further than saying, that they must be thoroughly good. I know nothing more injured by inferior or adulterated food than birds; and it is, moreover, extravagant, as they waste more than they eat.

The rape-seed is often recommended to be soaked. In this case, it should be placed in an earthen jar, with about twice its own quantity of water, covered up near the fire, for about twelve hours. The water should be then poured off, and the seed dried on a sieve. The birds will not touch it as long as it is wet.

Hemp-seed is often the better for being bruised; that is, just slightly cracked; for very young birds, which chiefly live on it till after their first moult, this bruising is quite essential.

12. In full-grown birds, unless they are feeding their young or moulting, or have remarkably weak bills, it is better, I think, to put on the drag of cracking, rather than letting them swallow the seed as fast as they can do it. It is very amusing to see the Goldfinches busy with a hemp-seed; they generally go up on the perch to eat it, and after a little rapid turning the seed about they shut up their mouths completely, and sit regarding you with the most preternatural air of occupation and consideration. While, however, you are speculating (as you suppose the bird is) on the consequences of a bolt, suddenly the seed reappears, and you find the delay had only been in the hope that the seed would soften. We may suppose it does, for the next proceeding is to place various pieces with elaborate care on the perch, which then quickly (and finally) disappear. I have had birds deposit the precious morsels on my fingers many a time, to be taken care of while they eat the rest. Bread crumbs are very good for all birds as a change of food. I think that stale bread grated is the best way to give it.

Melon seeds, chopped up fine, are often extremely
beneficial when a bird has a cold, or seems to be
suffering under any change of diet. The Cantaloupe
melon is the best kind, as far as I know, to give them.
Lettuce seed also is sometimes good.

The food should always be given early in the day,
and it is better not to mix one very favourite seed
with the rest, as it is then thrown about so much. I
often strew the hemp, for instance, upon the floor, or
give it from my own hand. The seed-box, &c. should
be thoroughly cleaned out constantly, and a small
sieve is very useful for removing dust, and any loose
husks can be blown away, and the good seed returned
into the box.

13. It is well to make a great point of seeing at
night, that the birds have food enough for next morning's breakfast if it is daylight long before they are
fed, I have known great injury done by forgetfulness of
birds' early habits; and a few hours waiting for food
in the morning, especially in the case of nestlings, is
most severely felt. Very often, indeed, it gives
a check from which they do not recover. A bird's
day, it must be remembered, is from sunrise to sunset. In the case of poultry, for example, the principal
difficulty attending winter broods lies in the long
night, during which the chickens are exposed to
remain unfed.

Chapter VII.

TREATMENT OF BIRDS WHEN SICK.

1. It is utterly miserable to read the long lists given of the birds' diseases and their so-called remedies.

Plenty of preventive measures there might be rightly, and a little nursing, for a sick bird is not generally kindly treated by its own companions; but I own that a case which goes beyond a bath or a warm wrap, a piece of liquorice or a rusty nail, a little groundsel, or some watercresses, is generally, in my opinion, not very likely to be improved by a lady's doctoring.

Up to that point, there is a little margin for a small sort of quackery.

2. First, there are " wooden shoes," which I confess I find great delight in curing; it is so pleasant to see the birds' relief when the load falls off. This discomfort arises from a damp or dirty cage, or one not sufficiently supplied with clean red sand; when the feet become gradually perfectly clogged with a sort of dirty shoe, sounding very much, indeed, as if the bird wore sabots; and when a bird is bought in such a state, it is a legitimate case for attempting a cure immediately. Take a saucer containing luke-warm soft water, not hot, but milk-warm; and then carefully catching the bird in one hand, cause it

to stand for at least five minutes if possible in its shallow bath. To take hold of the bird without hurting it, it is very essential to keep the hand quite *outside* the wings ; watching an opportunity for lightly closing it when the bird has both its wings folded. It is best to keep the head over the thumb ; and as the feet are very often tucked up just when we want them down, the mistress's hand is usually forced to take a bath with the bird. Jenny, one of my pets, was extremely bad when I got her ; but after three days of this treatment, she was as comfortable as could be ; and considering how she pecked and screamed at being caught at first, it was very amusing to witness her complacency as her shoes wore out. I always present the patients with hempseeds while in the bath ; sometimes they only hold them (taking them back to their cage to eat) ; but at any rate it assures them that people who give them such delicious things, cannot possibly mean harm.

There should be always a little bed of rather fine dry oatmeal for the bird to stand on for a moment when its bath is over ; this dries the feet, and in all ways is useful, while its dusting the feathers does not the slightest harm.

But except in the case of birds very newly bought, this is treatment not likely ever to be required, as clean cages and clean sand are sufficient preservatives from this discomfort as well as from the one which I will mention in case of a similar need.

3. I once bought two birds at the door which were evidently made very uncomfortable by a torment arising from want of bathing—very minute red insects like cheese mites, which were amongst their feathers. These birds were twice dusted with Dumont's or Keating's insect powder, taking care that the powder did not get into their eyes; and after the second time of dusting, the patients appeared quite well. They bathed, at the same time, frequently, their cage was well scrubbed daily with yellow soap and water : but newly-bought birds, for fear of such annoyances, should never be mixed at first with others, unless they are obtained from a dealer on whom one can depend.

4. Some birds, more particularly Canaries, have a talent for taking cold, and are heard conversing in the hoarsest tones. For this a piece of Spanish liquorice about the size of a pea, dropped into the water glass, is a very simple remedy. If, however, it is left there long, I always give a second glass of clean water after a short time in the morning, as the birds soon begin to dislike the taste if they have nothing else to drink. My birds the other day, some light-coloured Canaries, thought proper to wash in this cough mixture; the effect was not ornamental, but I suppose less injurious in the end than most cosmetics are.

Watercress is invaluable for keeping birds in good health : indeed, they are not often ill while they are kept clean, free from draughts, well supplied with this favourite salad, and *not* crammed with all sorts of trash.

·5. It is very essential also to see that their seed is good, that it is bright and well-filled, and that it has not been where mice can get near it, for mice seem in all ways great enemies of birds. I do not know how it is, but the terror birds have of them is singularly great. My very favourite Goldfinch was killed last winter by a mouse one night running round the cage, the cold probably having made it bold, and bird seed being tempting : before I could take the poor little fellow in my hand, it had fallen down on the floor of the cage quite dead. It might be from fluttering too hard against the bars, or, as I thought, from a fit. When a bird is sitting, mice are very dangerous if they get up to the nest.

6. Sometimes, especially if a bird builds early in the year while the weather is cold, she will be subject to a sort of fit when she begins to lay her eggs or sits ; probably cold weather renders her much more exhausted. In the cold spring this year, one of my birds was very ill indeed ; she lay on her side with all her feathers fluffed out, and did not even stir when her mate in the excess of his affectionate disquietude perched himself on her shoulder,

and setting his feet firmly together, took her wing in his beak and tugged it with all his might to induce her to get up. I thought such nursing, however, might be dispensed with, so having got some warm water, and with exceedingly great care given the bird a bath (of course holding her in my hand the while), I wrapped her up, insensible as she was, in a very warm piece of flannel, and having kept her warm all day, I had the pleasure at night of seeing her eating crumbs of sponge biscuit (which was her favourite refreshment,) with considerable appetite. She has never, I am sure, forgotten that day's nursing, for she is the only bird who now makes no fuss at all if I take her up. The others kick and scratch and peck as hard as they can, maintaining firmly the difference between being taken, and coming of themselves.

7. The moulting is always a trying time to birds; the young ones lose their first feathers at about three months old, the old ones generally about August or September. At this time they require warmth, and as they have little appetite, it is better to give them as much variety in their food as possible, also being careful to crush for them any hard kind of seed like hemp, as they are very weak. A rusty nail or a shred of saffron in the water glass is a useful tonic. And if the bird should be attacked with any sort of fit, some authorities recommend dipping its feet in warm

water, others, much less safely, giving it a bath of cold; but I do not think anything is better than laying the bird down on a marble slab, which gives it a shock of cold without making it wet, and when it comes to itself keeping it very warm in a well-heated flannel.

8. One of my original pair of Canaries used, I remember, to distress me every spring and autumn by a succession of what seemed very violent fits. Yet she lived for years, and was the mother each summer of a goodly family. A little oatmeal, a lump of chalk, and a piece of bay salt, are all very desirable to keep in the cage, as the birds have thus an opportunity to re-sort to their natural remedies, if they feel indisposed.

9. Birds are extremely apt to suffer by any sudden change of food, as well as by exposure to cold, damp, fatigue, or fright. In all these cases the nearer the food can resemble the natural kind the better, and I have already said how important it is in buying a new bird to hear exactly what food it has had, the food being so much a matter of individual habit, which seems often to take the place of that which is most natural to the class. As a general rule, how-ever, I think that canary seed, with a little new rape, hemp, and flax, will suit; hard-boiled egg is also a very good thing for birds when moulting, weak, or ill, and I often have given mine a little cold milk to drink, or have fed them with scalded bread, which

has been beaten up, after pouring off the water, with some cold milk and maw or poppy seed, of which most birds are fond. This small seed scattered amongst the sand is also invaluable for teaching young birds to peck. For a sick Goldfinch thistle and groundsel seeds are the best kind of food, and very generally a few ants' eggs are good and strengthening. They can be kept dry in sand all the winter, and softened by hot water.

10. Young birds are excessively liable to a disease which resembles that called in poultry "the gapes," though it does not seem to be at all the same thing in reality. The bird mopes and is uncomfortable, ruffles up its feathers, and keeps opening its bill as if it wanted air. The bill is generally dry and yellowish underneath the eyes, and the bird has a generally miserable look about it suggestive of its real disease, an exceedingly bad cold. Some strong black *tea* without milk, linseed, poppy seed, plenty of green stuff, and a little liquorice in the water, are amongst the best remedies, but perfect warmth is the greatest requisite. I think this complaint is contagious, and, therefore, should always recommend removing any other birds from the same cage, or if in an aviary, placing the sick bird in hospital.

11. It is a very great thing to make young birds wash properly; in pluming themselves afterwards they are forced to have recourse to the provision

made for oiling their feathers and keeping them waterproof, and this prevents, at the same time, cold-catching, from wet penetrating the feathers, and inflammation, often accompanied by a painful spot, that forms a little above the tail feathers from the accumulation of the oil. In the open air morning mists and summer showers soon compel the birds to attend to this duty, in-doors it is well to remind them of it by a gentle sprinkle from a brush or syringe, always choosing for this a time when the sun is shining. A little glycerine, or even cold cream, put on with a feather, is the best remedy, if any is required; but I think if the birds are taught to bathe, the disease will not often show itself.

12. One caution I must give most emphatically; it is, *never* to let young birds fly loose in a room for many weeks after they are fledged, unless they have been used to *hop* about in one before they can fly at all, or are brought out of the nest under parental care, when, of all sights connected with the aviary, one of the very prettiest is the young brood's early lessons. If, however, a little bird is let fly alone, it will fail in balancing its flight, so as continually to strike its head against the wall or ceiling; and if there are windows with the blinds drawn up, or glasses of any kind, it will most likely strike against them and hurt itself. I lost several beautiful little birds this year, entirely from the accident of their thus getting loose.

The best way to accustom a bird to fly when it is old enough to do so, is to let out a few of those who are quite accustomed to it, and then, having drawn down the blinds, or, still better, closed any muslin curtains, the bird will hop out of its cage peaceably, and when it has once examined the room well, will ware glass sufficiently.

13. If unfortunate accidents do, however, happen to birds getting loose, I think the best thing that can be done is merely to keep them wrapped up warmly for a day or two, feeding them with egg or milk from a quill, if their heads have been badly bruised, as often happens. Should they meet with a fall or blow so severe as to stun them in their rapid flight, a few moments generally is sufficient to bring them to themselves, and they must be held in the hand or put into a soft cage to recover, as otherwise they begin at once to beat about in a great fright: a little cold water dropped on the head and bill, is the best thing for them; and after such escapades, the cage should be shaded for an hour or two to give the patient a little time to rest, when, if it is not seriously injured, it will soon be again quite comfortable.

14. In case these disasters happen, I think it is always well to have a cage fitted up suitably for a hospital. I prefer a low sort of double-sized trap-cage, the wire sides being all taken out, and a piece of canvas or flannel, bound or hemmed all round,

being nailed or sewn in their place. The top of thin netting should take on and off, and there should be no perch, or only one placed at one end, and very low. A soft bed of very fine moss or flannel seems to me the best for the bird to lie on ; but anything thready or hairy must carefully be avoided, as a bird is always apt to get its feet and wings entangled.

If the cage is tolerably roomy there will perhaps be space for a shallow bath, which I always fancy relieves the bird, the head, at any rate, getting a refreshing wash, and certainly very often the ailing limb being also cooled by a little sprinkling.

The seed and food the bird usually has should be abundantly supplied, and placed in such a manner that it can help itself both to food and water from the same position : a good deal of seed may also be on the floor. Plenty of green stuff—watercress, chickweed, and groundsel—should be always given on these occasions, and sand in some shallow receptacle, if there is no room for it on the cage floor, as usual, and much best. Warmth also, and perfect quiet, are great things at these times, and though there should be a shady corner, darkness is not generally desirable, as it depresses the bird and worries it. Of course the patient should be always fed and cared for by its chief friend in the family ; attention to this one thing saving a world of fluttering.

15. While, however, a non-doctoring system is

doubtless, as far as ladies are concerned, the best; when any serious accident does happen, or when a bird is very ill, it is so natural to long to alleviate the pain, or to prolong the bird's really happy life, that I must not conclude this chapter without naming a bird dealer devoted apparently, as so many Germans are, to the pursuit he has followed in a humble fashion since he was a boy of seven. His name is Litolff, 25, Rose Street, Long Acre, and he seems to me to be well acquainted with birds and their ailments. I understand he is very successful as a bird doctor, and mender of broken limbs; and I may here remark that a canary of my own hatched and brought up large families for several succeeding years after the unlucky accident which deprived her of a leg.

16. A strange cat last winter by some extraordinary means made its way into my room one evening in the twilight, and before I knew of its presence, it had sprung upon and knocked down a cage from a table near. One bird flew away unhurt, but the other was injured by the falling cage, and had its leg broken. It was taken up and given to me quite gently, and without even attempting then to examine the injury, I laid it in a cage just such as I described, and kept it close beside me for the next ten days : talking to it seeming to comfort and amuse it mightily. The leg was stiff and useless for a long time after, but when once it had begun

5

to bathe, the recovery was rapid, and the bird now is a very fine and healthy one, and has built and hatched this summer.

It is very touching the way the sick birds cling to one in their troubles; they lie looking at one for help so pitifully, taking so gently the offered food, and always seeming disposed to nestle so closely to one. After all I have said, however, I can but repeat my conviction that cleanliness, watercress, and abstinence from *messes* are the best means of preserving a bird in health; and if, after all, it does become ill, keeping it very warm—not roasted before the fire, but nestled in snugly—is the best mode of both comforting and curing it.

CHAPTER VIII.

BREEDING IN AVIARIES.

1. THE most enjoyable arrangement that I ever knew for the cage birds building, was a plan adopted for my birds, when I was a child. In some little details I may perhaps make mistakes; but as the birds belonged to me, and always were great pets, I do not think that any important thing will have been forgotten.

We had at that time a good many birds kept in

different ways, some loose in a room, some in single cages, and others in one large cage standing about six feet high, which was divided into separate apartments, and provided with gratings to shut off young broods.

This cage used every spring to be carried out into the garden, when the greenhouse plants went, and there it stood under a beautiful scarlet Thorn till the first cold days of autumn warned us to take it back to its winter quarters in the hall, near enough to the fire to be kept pretty warm.

2. In a cage of this size, if birds of only one or two kinds are kept, there may be as many as ten or a dozen pairs. We generally had a few Linnets and Goldfinches, and all the rest Canaries; and all these used to pair a good deal, Canaries with Goldfinches, and so on.

There is always a doubt as to the good agreement of many birds together; but it must be remembered that two birds alone in a cage will fight, if it so pleases them, just like cat and dog; while in an aviary, or large-sized cage, the space for flight and for dodging is far greater if they do fight; and it is very rare that more than a single bird at once will attack another. When a whole cage full *do* set themselves against one luckless individual, the only thing for it is to give him another home. But a great deal depends on careful management; letting the birds be well acquainted, at least by sight and hearing, before they actually share the same cage; letting them loose together, above all when they are not hungry, and consequently cross.

Many persons would have as many, perhaps, as eighteen hen birds to half a dozen cocks; but I have said already that, for my own part, out of the poultry yard, I have no faith in such Turks. The numerous wives very often rob one another's nests; or else they fight, instead of sitting quietly. An absurd little Canary hen of mine, for instance, invariably flies off her nest in the most reckless manner, and goes dashing off after her most particular enemy, if she even so much as sees her passing; and of course these sudden antics are very dangerous both for eggs and young.

3. One very great consideration to those who keep birds for pleasure, is assuredly the happiness of the tribe; and who would like to lose that prettiest of sights when the forwardest nestling arrives first at the perch, and sits between its parents fluttering its little wings and being fed by them alternately, in the midst of busy and delighted twittering. Of course when one bird is father of about four young families, there is not much chance of his being much at home with any of them; and the mother has no business to be always off her nest, as she must really be, to supply a strong brood all by herself,

with food. I have been confidently assured by long
experienced bird-keepers, that even where number
is the great object, as in their own case (breeding
young birds for sale), the trying for too many often
ends in the loss of all. A general skirmish terminates
in torn nests, or, even supposing that peace is main-
tained, a general weakness ensues amongst all the
birds, the old ones being over-worked, and the
young ones under-fed. Cheerfulness, too, is an important thing in a birdcage, and a poor little hen
toiling on all alone is by no means a lively sight.

For peace, then, for happiness, and even for
numbers to be reared, I strongly advise my readers
to match their birds pretty fairly, withdrawing any
member who is decidedly black-balled, and giving
opportunity before entering the aviary of forming a
slight acquaintance.

4. After February or March it is rather a risk to
introduce new inmates into an aviary already arranged
for breeding. If one of a pair should die, it is best
to remove the mate till it has formed another match;
when the pair *may* be put in again, though with some
risk of the new bird not agreeing with those which
were there before.

An entirely new pair can be put in with more
safety, but we always need to have a few single cages
for such birds as are separated from the others for
any cause whatever.

I shall not, then, attempt to enter at any length into the uncomfortable fashion alluded to just now. I believe where it is attempted it is usual to have a cage with several partitions, a nest box in each, and as soon as one bird begins to sit, her mate is taken away, and she is left to bring up her brood alone.

5. In one instance proceedings like these may be rendered necessary. If a Goldfinch and Canary build together, the Goldfinch is sometimes disposed to break his poor wife's eggs ; probably because they are not exactly the colour he expects to see them. But all are not so cruel ; and Goldfinches sometimes bring up young families in a most exemplary manner. I have myself one so good-natured that, having no family of his own this year, when a poor little strange "grey pate" fluttered its wings and looked up at him in a meek and insinuating way, he actually fed it and comforted it, as though it had been his own. There are, however, varieties of disposition. But the general caution is quite necessary: that if birds of different races pair, when the eggs naturally look different, it is always necessary to look sharply after them as soon as they are laid ; if, for instance, it is certain that the hen *has* laid, and yet no egg is visible, it would be safer next day to lock up the suspected party behind the sliding grating till the expected egg is safely in our possession, when it can be put into another nest for hatching.

6. Birds do not, however, generally approve of any interference, and the less they undergo, the better they will succeed.

Some persons make a practice of taking away the eggs in all cases, as fast as they are laid, thereby losing a great many birds. Others dip them in warm water; others sprinkle them to aid in the hatching: but all these practices are worse than useless, and if they were required the bird herself would see to it.

Chaffinches, for instance, in hot weather have been noticed damping their eggs with water in their bills; and when the eggs are bad, the hen generally finds it out, and thereupon leaves the nest.

7. It is a very necessary thing that plenty of light and air should be afforded, whether in the aviary or in breeding-cages.

I dislike the practice of hanging cages, as people often do, by the side of a window, to be out of the strong light. The nest itself, doubtless, should be in a shady corner, and either a spray of leaves or a piece of green baize may be hung over the spot where it is being built; but of all depressing things to the old birds, and of all hurtful and weakening things for the young, the absence of direct light and of the warm soft rays of the morning sun, are the worst to which they can be exposed. Some young birds, in fact, leave their nests less than half fledged from this very cause, as nothing adds so much to the quick

growth of the feathers as the warm (not scorching)
sunshine, such as flickers down through the leaves
of some waving shrub ; and the fresh air and moisture
of the summer dew help the nestlings both in their
growth and feathering.

Thus it was that our birds throve so well with their
nurseries out of doors. They had the early sunlight,
the sweet morning air, the dew, and the cheerfulness of
everything around, all keeping them well and happy,
till, indeed, I should now be quite afraid to say how
many young birds, year by year, used to grow up
with us.

8. When there was a young family old enough to
leave the maternal wing, a small cage would be provided, or a division of the aviary prepared for them.
In whichever they were placed, we took care they
should have plenty of little round holes (like those
miserable holes for getting at seed and water), which
they could be fed through if their parents pleased.
We used always to strew a good deal of crushed
hemp, and maw seed, and crumbs of stale bread,
upon the floor of the cage, as soon as ever the young
ones began to leave their nest and to hop about, so
that afterwards, the same plan being continued in
their own new cage, half the difficulty of teaching
them to eat was obviated.

It is a good thing to accustom young birds to be
very clean : baths in fine weather are not likely to be

hurtful ; but if they do not wash, a little sprinkling from a fine brush is sometimes desirable to force them to preen their feathers. To be in a cage in view of the old birds is often helpful here, and at any time I would gladly give up one hatch of birds for the sake of the pleasure it is to see the little fledglings getting their education—the parental scoldings, pecks, and pokes which are so amusing.

9. Unless a set of birds are already on a very familiar footing with their mistress and extremely tame, it does not do to seem to watch them much. At the same time when a young pair bred up from nestlings, or long become tame, have begun to build, they will often go on composedly, and allow of almost any amount of friendly interference.

I suspected the other day that one of mine had been building a floorless nest, and put a finger into the nest to see : both birds came immediately, and, standing at the door to watch me, gave no sign of fear or of displeasure, but simply wished to know what I could be at. A very soft, well-felted lining, after all, I found, and directly I removed my finger, into her nest popped the little bird, and there she sat amidst her fir branches, with her little black eyes glittering as I hardly thought a bird's eyes would glitter ; she also took crumbs of biscuits or of hemp seed when I held them to her, with evident satisfaction.

10. When imported birds breed in England, it is very amusing to witness their determined adherence to the ways of their own land. There is a most curious instance of this given in Jesse's *Gleanings*, of an African bird—one of the Cardinal Grosbeaks—which was put into the same cage with a hen Goldfinch, in order to try if they would breed together; they did so, and the hen having begun to sit, the tropical bird took a quantity of grass and covered her up with it. This he did regularly every day at eleven o'clock (at which time the sun came upon the cage), apparently for the purpose of screening the hen from the heat, and it was supposed that this attention was usual in the country from which the bird was brought.

Parrots, again, will insist on "a hollow tree" wherein to form their nest; the most successful broods are therefore reared in old barrels half full of sawdust, and with holes cut in the sides.

Goldfinches cannot bear building low down in a room; about the top of the curtain pole is the lowest level that they like. Many of the English wild birds, too, often will not build in an open cage (the Goldfinches generally, amongst others, will not), but they will build in a thick hedge of fir, or box, or gorse, if this is arranged for them in a room, or in an aviary cage, affording sufficient space.

Having made these stray remarks on the subject generally, I will now proceed to give a few rules as to

the little that has to be done for the birds in regard
to their building.

11. I have no faith at all in match-making; in nine
cases out of ten it is quite certain that the birds suit
themselves better than we could suit them. Besides,
half the amusement is seeing what they will do. The
prettiest nest I have had this year was the production
of a strong-minded female, who fairly hunted down a
poor little German bird not more than half her size.
Never was anything more amusing than Jenny's
pertinacity; first she drove away all the other birds,
daring them to come near her, and then she fairly
flattered little timid Tuft into becoming her most
submissive spouse. She treated him well, however,
and fought his battles for him.

12. A match between a Goldfinch and yellow
(Jonquille) Canary is one much to be desired; the
nestlings are so pretty. Siskins and Canaries are
also very pretty; and some of the little crimson
plumaged foreign birds should be encouraged in any
such alliances. The being together much, the being
thoroughly tame, and the having abundant room, and
good choice of building places, are the chief means by
which one might promote this end.

Two crested birds should never be allowed to pair.
I settle that by having with the others only crested
hens. The crested Goldfinches are extremely pretty
as well as rare, but I never heard of any progeny

from a crested Canary and Chaffinch. Crested Bullfinches are not desirable, as crests never suit those
large-headed, thick-billed birds. The young of a
Canary and Linnet are very pretty; but not equal,
I think, to those of Goldfinches or Siskins and Jonquille Canaries.

13. Branches or trees in pots should be put into
the cage, room, or aviary, as early as possible for the
birds to get used to them; but in the chapters on
Rooms, Aviaries, and Cages, I will describe more fully
the various ways of arranging these.

14. About the end of March is quite early enough
to begin to furnish nest materials. In a very early
spring I have known the birds begin to build in
February; but as we cannot ensure warm weather for
the young birds' early growth, about four weeks later
when they should leave the nest, it seems the safer
plan not to encourage these very early broods.

It does not, on the other hand, answer when they
begin to sit very late, because then the second or
third brood is apt to be made too backward.
About six weeks generally elapse from the time of
the first sitting till the next begins. And it is very
common to have four or five broods of Canaries in a
season. The wild birds in Madeira begin to build in
February, and hatch quite as often, though Linnets
and Goldfinches hatch generally only twice a year.

15. When the birds are about to build, a few little

bags of network should be prepared, filled with small tufts of soft dry moss or grass, free from stalks, a little soft hair or wool, which is better *short*, as a long hair sometimes gets caught about a bird's foot; a few nice little feathers, also, are a great boon, and some soft down or thistle-down is best for the lining. I should observe here, too, that birds are particular in their tastes: one prefers a white lining, and another a brown, and so far are they from conforming their tastes to their means, that if they cannot have the one preferred they often will not have any. As, however, it is very much safer for the young to be warmly housed, a little trouble in humouring their mamma will not be thrown away. Feathers, I always fancy, answer best for Canaries, many of the Warblers, Titmice, Wrens, &c.; their own little *wild* nests are perfect depths of warm, soft, downy feathers. But in all these things birds differ: Goldfinches prefer hair, and Thrushes think mud more suitable, and a dishonest Sparrow, living on our lawn, once stole a piece of flannel from the nursery window, and we afterwards found it nestling with it in a large clipped yew-tree !

I think it better to give two bags, putting that with the moss in first; but if the birds are in cages the bags should be hung outside the wires, to prevent, not only entanglements, but considerable waste of strength; as in the case of two of mine, when they dragged up forcibly the whole bag to their nursery, into which it would not enter, the door being rather narrow. When I think of the Herculean labours of those two small creatures, I always feel wicked for not having prevented it. I suspect Jenny thought she was conveying her nest up wholesale, and that she meant to jump upon it and to scoop out a hole.

16. It is very common to buy nest bags ready fitted up, and, for once, it may be well to see the sort of stuff they are made of. It will, probably, however, be advisable to put the bags aside unused, as they are generally scented with powder of some kind—unpleasant, I think, to both birds and owners, and certainly not natural for the former. The nest bags are important items, as so much of the comfort of the brood depends on their good supply and perfect cleanliness. It is absolutely essential to have all bought materials thoroughly baked or scalded before they are used.

17. The Canary often begins sitting from the day on which her first egg is laid, thus beginning to hatch in thirteen days after. Some people "take care" of the eggs for the unhappy birds; but I am sure that the rule of letting things alone answers much the best here, and the deserted nests and the uncared-for young are not usual in the woods and fields—they are events reserved for places where "every possible pains is taken."

Four living nestlings used, with us, to be no uncommon thing, but then we were not too helpful;
we saw that there was always food at hand, and once,
when the hen bird died and the cock seemed perplexed
as to how he was to act nurse, we undertook to help
him, and by feeding endlessly from early morning to
quite the evening, we certainly contrived to rear a tame
and pretty set of little downy birds.

18. The birds, sometimes, after building properly,
will, without any apparent cause, coolly fill up the
nest, generally with some white stuff, and quietly
forsake it. This is generally when they have been
disturbed by strangers, or when the eggs are addled.
The latter is sometimes the case after a thunder-
storm, a door slamming violently, or some such cause.

I do not think that after the nest has been once
filled up they often return to it. I should, in such
cases, therefore, take the birds into another room or
aspect if they are in a cage; at any rate, removing the
whole machinery, box, or branch, or whatever it may
be, of the other nest, and giving facilities for making
a fresh start. The nest may, however, in some cases,
be left as it is, when it would be troublesome to remove it; but deserted nests are bad nooks for insects,
and a bird is all the better for not being reminded of
its former failure.

19. Some birds are first-rate sitters and nurses,
others very careless, and while these need constant

watching, they are very often also the least familiar, and the most ready to take offence. The penalty, too, of their negligence is serious in the first days of hatching, no less than murdered nestlings. After a little practice, however, the general look of things shows if all is right. A real good bird for sitting and bringing up her young is a great acquisition, and should always have every advantage, and should she even be an inferior bird she would be invaluable, with first-rate eggs substituted for her own.

If the hen bird should have fits while sitting, as is very likely, especially in cold weather, it is best to put her very gently in a warm bath ; laying her afterwards on a piece of heated flannel. The greatest care is necessary, however, not to hurt the bird while holding it in the hands.

20. While birds are sitting, the supply of food should always be very abundant. I am doubtful myself if the hard-boiled egg is really a good addition ; bread, well baked, and allowed to get rather stale, answers very well mixed with pounded hemp-seed—some say pounded rape—and Mr. Kidd, who is a great authority in these matters, recommends bread and milk. In that case the bread should be finely grated, and *cold* milk poured on just enough to moisten it. My birds have, nevertheless, often done very well with no change from their ordinary food, except an additional allowance of pounded hemp, with a little maw-seed.

Some old pounded mortar in the cage is essential, and a rusty nail in the water glass. Plenty of chick-weed, too, is a great advantage.

Where egg is given, I should much recommend its being finely pounded, and mixed with the grated bread. Only a small quantity should be given at a time, and it should never be left to get sour in the cage.

21. Cleaning a breeding-cage is an immense difficulty. It is a very good plan to cover the floor *thickly* at first with sand, and then, if absolutely necessary, the top may be raked off; having what the cage-makers call *a slide* is, for this, an advantage, even above a drawer. Drawers are open to the very grave objection that they afford so convenient a harbour in which insects may lodge. But when slide cages are used in common, there should be a spare one, that they may be well cleaned by turns.

22. It is desirable to have a small cage *hooked on* to contain seed and water. There is generally a small door whereon it can be hung, and it makes a wonderfully great difference in the neatness of the cage. These suggestions must not be despised because they seem so trivial, for when any one tries to keep a cage both clean and quiet for five weeks, it will be found to be no such easy task.

23. In cages it is also a good plan to put a few soft little sprays of foliage into the building-place in which the nest is to be; the little yellow head, with its

6

bright eyes peeping out, is so extremely pretty half seen amidst the green.

24. The day before the young are expected to be hatched, some grated bread, and a finely-chopped up hard-boiled egg should be put in the cage in a saucer. This should *always* be given in the evening an hour before the bird's usual roosting time, and again in the morning as early as it can be done conveniently. It is not essential to do this at sunrise—eight or nine o'clock will do ; but then the evening supply must never be omitted, as its object, of course, is to provide for the early hours, before the rest of the world are up, although the small birds are.

25. Nothing conduces more to the young birds' health than being in a spot which catches the rising sun. If they do not feather quickly it is rather a good plan to sprinkle them sometimes on a warm sunny morning with a few drops of water from a soft brush, but if the old birds bathe this will not be necessary.

As to the feeding of the young when they leave the nest, to have pounded hemp, bread-crumbs and seed scattered about the floor, is all I need recommend ; till we come to the time when, the parents being engaged with another nest, the poor little fledglings have to be taken from them ; even then, however, their being sent to reside in a cage that touches the old birds' home, affords opportunity for the latter, if they are so disposed, still to take notice of them.

Chapter IX.

REARING YOUNG BIRDS.

1. In bringing in nests of young birds to rear with the
parents' help, I think it is always best to choose such
families as are already tolerably tame;—when, for
instance, any one has been in the habit of feeding a
certain brood, or of conversing much with the old
birds as they hop on the window-ledge, or upon the
turf, before one. The great thing is in this to avoid
anything that is of a scaring nature. Birds have
frequently been known to build in the hats of scare-
crows; so it is not that exactly, which I mean here:
but the glittering cages, and those that shut with a
jar, or which have a door which slams to when
touched; noisy cages, again, with a ringing wire; all
these things are often much more alarming than
any dressed-up figures.

2. The younger the birds are when removed, the
better, after they have once got over the three or four
first days. The proper way, then, of proceeding, is to
procure a cage with no *glitter* whatever about it, a
mere wicker one if fine enough, or a dark green fine-
wired one. The door should be large, and made to
open in the front; it is all the better if it hooks on
and off. Having decided on the nest which we mean
to have, it is a good plan to nearly fill the cage with

little branches of the same kind of tree as that in which the nest is ; then a few days at latest before the young birds are fledged, the cage should be hung in the tree itself, or in one close by, and the twigs that keep the nest in its place being very carefully cut off with it or else detached from it with even greater caution, the nest may be placed inside the cage prepared for it. For the two or three first days, the old birds may be allowed to go in and out without any interference. The next move should be to bring the cage into a shady window or into a conservatory, carefully providing against any risk of shutting out the parent birds at night. It is also well to give a little help now and then in the feeding, before removing, even from the time of the young birds being nearly able to see (they cannot see for the first week), and by giving a little sopped bread or biscuit every now and then by means of a rounded quill, they are prepared for bringing up by hand, if by any contretemps the parents should forsake them.

3. As the little birds begin to hop about, the most difficult time approaches. Sometimes a very kind old bird will take the young brood in hand and teach them pecking ; but more frequently the nestlings are left to our care, for it is impossible to imprison the poor old birds, whose love for their brood brings them near that danger.

4. The seed for young birds should be strewed on

a sanded floor. Crushed hemp is in almost all cases
the best food at first for Finches and such like. And
this should be mixed with a good share of stale bread-
crumbs, merely crumbled up, not soaked. Maw seed
is often particularly useful in teaching birds to pick
up, and it is essential always at night to leave abundant food for the next day's breakfast.

The sooner the little birds will wash the better for
them ; and their cage should never be without green
food, chickweed, groundsel, or watercresses, which, in
London at least, can be obtained all winter.

5. A hard-boiled egg, white and yolk finely chopped
up together, is useful for these little birds. It must,
however, be constantly given fresh.

A rather novel and exceedingly useful remedy is a
little strongish tea, when the birds seem sickly. It
should be left in the cage as well as some fresh water ;
the birds then can take it or not, as their instinct
leads them, and when they are weakly, or liable to
cold, it often is good for them.

The more sunshine these young things can have
the better ; one end and the back of the cage being
partly covered, they can find shade if necessary, and
if the weather is hot, a branch or two of an evergreen
makes a nice trembling shade, in which they all
delight.

6. In rearing these little creatures, a great deal
depends on obtaining the food they are accustomed to

have when wild. Thistle seed, dandelion seed, plantain, besides groundsel and chickweed, and, perhaps most important of all, some insects; ants' eggs are the pleasantest to give them, as they are only eggs; but aphides and most sorts of insects are welcome. Goldfinches, in spite of their character for only eating seeds, are very glad of insects for a change, especially for their young, and so are Canaries, Bullfinches, and *the whole*, in fact, of the great Sparrow (or Passerine) class. When these birds are reared by hand, the food given should be rather moist, as the old birds feed from the bill, moistening the food in their own mouths first. I have found hard-boiled egg pounded (always white and yolk) and mixed with a little water, to answer very well; but it should be remembered, that the old birds bring them whatever they can catch, and that thus they have a constant change of food, which is extremely serviceable. Pounded mortar or lime rubbish is very good to have mixed with the sand. Egg-shells calcined and ground answer the purpose perfectly.

7. The little chicks are extremely funny, they are so marvellously conceited and bold. One fledgling I have now, will take to roosting on the middle of a perch, and will let no one else intrude upon him there; and as there are only four high perches in my cage, and more than twenty birds, it may be supposed that a considerable fuss ensues.

These birds, however, make nothing of attacking anything : I have myself seen small Grey-pates hop boldly forward and assault a bird the size of a small Pigeon, so that I am quite unwilling to trust these imprudent small birds any longer in the same cage with large ones till they have grown older and more wise.

8. A deep bed of moss, covered with wool, and with a small *blanket,* daily changed for a clean one, is the best arrangement for the nest. The flannel should cover the young birds up completely, and only be taken off for food to be given, which should be done very often, from sunrise to sunset. Every hour is *best,* every two hours is almost necessary ; and they eat several (about four) quillfuls at each meal. A few drops of water should be also given, one or so occasionally between the supplies of food. It is very desirable to give some peculiar call or whistle before uncovering the birds to feed, repeating it often while giving them their food. If they are to learn to whistle tunes, they will thus acquire a habit of association which will be very useful.

9. When it is difficult to make them eat, the imitation of the old bird's note will often cause them to do so. It is an important thing, too, to notice *how* the old birds give the food ; some putting their own bill into the chick's, and others standing up tall and dropping the dinner into the gaping mouth. This should be imitated as nearly as possible.

Canaries and Goldfinches put in their bills like
Doves; Robins, Thrushes, &c. tumble the food down
their offsprings' throats.

10. I doubt if very young birds can eat too much.
The chief danger, I think, is in their getting too little
food—too little nourishment in what they do have,
and in the slightest exposure to either damp or cold.

11. The little birds moult at a very early age,
almost before they have got over their early troubles
and the learning to hop and fly. Extra warmth,
extra food, and extra quiet are at this time necessary.
If they survive September it may fairly be hoped
that they will do well.

12. Wonderfully tame these little pets grow. I
have one who follows my hand about the side of a
large cage just like a little dog, nestling up against
it, and putting its little claw out through the wires
to take hold of my fingers; and as to Bully and
Bobby, it is laughable to see how they sidle and bow,
and fluff out their fine red plumes, and go edging
along as long as one will talk to them.

One of the prettiest sights is a little bird request-
ing to be fed; it looks so pretty fluttering its wings
and putting up its head. Even in London I find
there is plenty to be seen of this sort, both in and
out of doors. A little Sparrow the other day in-
terested me extremely by hopping about by my
window in a great crowd of others, begging very

hard ; some were contemptuous ; some hopped away ;. but a few were kind and fed the little beggar. One of the most provoking of fledglings, however, is the cuckoo. I have been told by a person continually amongst woods that it is really touching to see the anxiety with which the poor Hedge Sparrow, after standing on tiptoe for many days to feed her giant nestling, is entirely overwhelmed when he first hops out to take the air by the enormous size and strength of that tender chick ; the poor little Sparrow is then seen hopping humbly after it, in the most ludicrous attitude of meekness and consternation.

Sometimes, when there is much difficulty in bringing up young birds, it even answers to hang the cage out of doors, observing the precautions I have already mentioned. As many as forty Sparrows have been seen bringing food, it is said, to a set of nestlings thus hung up in a cage, and I can speak by my own experience of the friendly feelings between the wild and tame birds.

In the country, of course, one expects the birds to be unsophisticated, but in London I confess that it would not have occurred to me to give those pert little Sparrows credit for such gentle ways.

CHAPTER X.

TEACHING YOUNG BIRDS TUNES.

1. It is fair to begin by saying that in this chapter I write only the experience of others, and what I have accidentally observed in watching their birds, for I have not yet myself given many music lessons. Having generally a good many birds with their natural song, it would have been necessary to banish them from my room, to prevent confusion amongst the scholars; and, besides, in most cases the sweet little warbler cannot well be improved upon. At the moment I write, however, I have some birds just going into training. The hints collected for their education may be useful to others, and, birds' ways being understood, such advice as is found to be theoretical can be rejected.

I never mean with my birds to try the starving system. There is no pleasure in making the bird unhappy, and it would only give a sad association to its little tune. My idea is always to play to them while they are at their breakfast, and after they have done eating—they are always then much more disposed to listen. After their bath again there is a grand twittering time while they are pluming themselves, and at bedtime there is always an amazing fuss, though I doubt if playing to them then would do any good.

2. I think myself birds learn best when they can be *whistled* to. A servant of my father's taught many birds in this way, and he followed no particular system, merely whistled the same tune at any spare moment, generally after or while he was feeding them.

3. Another bird, a Canary, possessed by some children I knew, was elaborately taught. The children had a little bird-organ, and each and all played "God save the Queen" on every occasion possible, until, although the bird was two or three years old, it learned to sing it beautifully, as also another ditty.

4. The earlier the birds are taken from the nest the freer their song will be, in all probability, from notes that are not wanted. The German trainers blow on the bird's feathers, and look cross, and scold it when it sings a wrong note, rewarding it with a hemp-seed or some such treat when it performs successfully. It generally takes several months to learn a tune perfectly. As a general rule those tunes which have a sort of running scale will be found the easiest and the most effective.

5. The organs of different birds are very various as well as their performances; but it is apparently a fact that the song of birds is not, strictly speaking, natural, but acquired at the very earliest age, from the notes of the parent singing near the nest; the knowledge of

this fact should be a great assistance in teaching birds to sing artificial songs.

The very general introduction into an acquired tune of a few of the bird's own notes, is most likely owing to its having been taken into training too far on in life ; even at four or five days old, when the nestlings cannot see, it appears they can remember the sound of the parent's voice ; probably, they listen to it alone, since, at this early age, it does not seem that they remember any other note, though birds of all sorts may be chirping round them. Any bird being taught either a tune or the song of another bird, should be kept in a cage alone and hung up, if possible, out of the sight of others ; it learns all the better for having its attention undisturbed from the notes that are being slowly played.

6. In teaching young birds to sing, *school* cages are useful, either a row of the little six-inch square cages, which seem to me the handiest, or else a long narrow box, wired in front and divided into compartments.

7. One really good singing bird—Woodlark, Nightingale, or Canary—may then be hung overhead and will teach them all. But we must beware of what companionship they have : learn they will whatever it is they hear, and so we had better provide them with a good instructor.

Even Sparrows may be taught to sing very well, not to mention talking. Bechstein speaks of two of these birds in Paris, who, in their frequent scuffles for food, used gravely to admonish one another, *Tu ne voleras pas.*

CHAPTER XI.
OCCUPANTS OF AN AVIARY.

1. Of all the knotty points in the keeping birds, the knottiest and the most troublesome is to know which will live together.

My own belief is that much more depends on the way of treatment than on the birds themselves. Of course, if a wild bird is put into a cage full of tame and gentle ones, it is much like a young gorilla set loose in a peaceful family: the mischief, the spite, the tricks, are something inconceivable,—every bird gets cross,—and the mistress is in despair. Civilized birds do not behave in this way, and it should be an unalterable law never to put a bird into an aviary, or large cage full of others, till it has been kept some days and has got used to the *place*. Birds are upset and bewildered by any change, as much or more than human beings; and the catching to put them in a travelling cage, and the journey,—being carried, perhaps, through some noisy streets,—is a disturbing business; and then, again, in the change of cages, very often, indeed, *new birds do not know where to look for the food and water.* Having once given the new-comers time to get perfectly at home with the room and their owner, and used to the faces and voices of those going in and out, the actual putting into the aviary is generally a very quiet work ; when in a single cage, too, they have wanted so much to be promoted to it !

2. In my experience of birds (speaking, of course, only of my own) I do not think that I have ever known one bird kill another. But there are a few kinds always excluded from the company, and at the building season I separate again those that are the larger, Bullfinches, Java Sparrows, &c., from the remainder. Bullfinches, however, are sometimes known to pair with Canaries ; chiefly in cases where they have been brought up together.

3. To continue the subject of birds that agree in aviaries, I must first remind my readers that three nests in one shrub, and those of different sorts, are by no means uncommon ; at least I have found them many a time thus placed : a very wide division does not then seem necessary. Still, of course, the wider the quarters are the more the cage resembles the open air with the numerous flocks of all sorts of wild birds we often see in places where they are cared for.

4. At this moment I have before me, living (for a time) in one large store cage, about three feet six long, by eighteen inches deep, a party of not less

than twenty birds. These have been put in three or
four at a time, and I always took care that they were
tolerably quiet before they were put in. There are
Canaries, Bullfinches, charming little Linnets, a
pretty Greenfinch, and an audacious little bird between
a Linnet and Canary who gives more trouble in
keeping peace than all the others together. The
rest of the party consists of Goldfinches, and very
pretty they look roosting in a long row with the
Linnets, seven in a line.

5. The cage at night stands in a passage, and is
covered well over with a woollen table-cloth. In the
day it stands in a window of my sitting-room on the
top of a plant case. A bath, glazed at the top and
three sides, is hooked upon the door, the amusement
of which is indescribable. Birds emerge at intervals
in parties of two or three, and go afterwards to " hang
themselves out to dry " on the sunniest perch or in
the swing, looking most wobegone. I have seen two
of these half-drowned creatures hanging out in the
swing together. The toilette that concludes the
business is very elaborate, and it is most amusing to
see the little Grey-pates, who want to have credit
for washing but do not like the cold, how they put in
one leg and pull it out again, and finally perch just
upon the edge while somebody else is washing, to
catch the shower sent up so vigorously. And then
the little cheat shakes itself out, makes an immense

to-do, and sometimes drives down a really washed bird from a sunny corner, that *it* may dry itself.

6. In a cage like this I find that the severest battles are between two Goldfinches; an old bird, for instance, and the boldest Grey-pate (one of this year's birds without the red head plumage); they scold, and flutter, and scream at one another, till it needs daily experience to feel easy that no harm will be done; still I never knew them to do more than make a tremendous noise.

7. The birds which are really unsafe (whatever may be the sweetness of their individual dispositions,) are Thrushes; Ox-eyes, or large Blue Tits; and Robins. I do not feel certain that Bobby would get fighting amongst other birds, only with fellow Robins, and in the glass with himself; still it seems to me to be a sort of waste to put Robins into a crowd, while with regard to other birds of the above-named classes it is really very necessary not to be misled by their innocent antecedents into admitting any. I heard of a Blue Tit, commonly called Tom Tit, who was hatched in a Canary's nest, and brought up always in a cage, and never had tasted anything stronger than bread and milk in all its life before; but a poor little brown mouse one day appeared in the room where Tom resided, and it was only "a word and a blow;" Tom made but one dash, and his victim lay dead upon the floor whilst very rapidly

were his brains devoured. This story illustrates only their natural instincts; but except under the closest supervision, Tom Tits should not be admitted; for, although they are the drollest of little birds, hanging on to everything, they hug other birds round the neck to rob them of the very bread or berry in their beaks in a way in which I should be sorry, indeed, to see any of my favourites hugged.

In an aviary in which we meant the birds to build, we had only Canaries, Linnets, Goldfinches, and Siskins. In a case like this, any *old* birds put in should be put in in pairs—even Goldfinches and Siskins, though, I believe, it is safer that their mates should be Canaries. Then, the young birds growing up may be left to take their own chance together.

8. In filling an aviary of six feet square or more, I should advise putting in birds in the following proportion :—

Two pairs of German Canaries, two Chaffinches, and two Bullfinches (both of these young birds). One pair of Linnets, rose or brown; two Siskins already paired with Canaries, half a dozen each of Grey-pates and young Linnets, four Siskins, and sixteen of the same year's Canaries.

In an aviary filled like this, there would be every probability of a great many very successful broods.

It is quite a case in which what succeeds with a few does with the many, and by keeping within

7

these proportions, I have very little doubt that with commonly good management the result would be satisfactory.

9. Of course any number less than that named would do quite as well or better, as it would give more room, or in increasing the number for a larger space, the proportions can be kept up; though I do not recommend any one to try more than fifty birds for the first beginning. In too great a multitude half the pleasure is lost of the clever tricks one sees played, by not being certain of the individuality of the culprits. For my own part I never wish to have more than two dozen grown-up birds at once.

10. It will of course be remarked that in my list for the aviary, I have excluded Warblers or the Sylvia; (Nightingales, Black-caps, Garden Warblers, Whitethroats, and many others of the same class of birds;) birds, that is, eating insects, seeking in winter a warm climate, and generally shy and very much given to avoid the approach of any stranger.

These birds are always difficult to keep, and, unless one of them has chanced to grow very tame and fond, the mere feeling of their unhappiness is enough to make their presence in cages painful.

Their misery when first caught is very great, and I do think it is a very cruel thing that they should be taken after they are once fledged. The young birds may get tame and be really happy; but it is probably hardly one in twenty of the old birds caught, that do.

I have had myself hardly any of this class, but having reared a few which came to grief by tumbling out of nests, till old enough to fly, I know that bread crumbs are generally the readiest food to give them. I prefer giving it dry or very nearly so, or beaten up with a little hemp-seed, or, still better, with a few drops of cold milk, an egg boiled hard and chopped extremely fine, *yolk and white together*, is also very good for them.

When they are once reared, German paste and stale bread-crumbs are the best staple foods for them; they like a great deal of water, and ought to have a very well sheltered cage, and a branch of a rose-tree covered with green fly is a most dainty feast.

Only one Nightingale ought to be kept at a time, as two will not often sing. It is very difficult to manage a Nightingale well, especially in an aviary which cannot be moved about. Some will sing in the light only, and others insist on shade; some cannot bear a noise to disturb them, and others sing the louder, warbling high above all the other notes.

Nightingales, too, require ants' eggs or insects to keep them in good song, and this is always a very great difficulty for a bird indoors.

All the warblers require a great deal of sand and water. Their food is best placed in shallow china dishes on the floor : hemp and canary seeds may also be strewn about ; the hemp need not be broken, as it is swallowed whole ; but the nearer we can approach the food they would have when wild the greater are always the chances of preserving them, both in health and song. It would be almost useless to give any list of these birds. Larks do not do well except in an outdoor aviary, and Whitethroats, Blackcaps and Garden Warblers give perhaps most chance of success, as well as being among the most desirable.

CHAPTER XII.

MAKING FRIENDS WITH WILD BIRDS.

1. It may seem at first as if to make friends with wild birds would be rather difficult, and also rather useless, yet it is really a pleasant branch of bird acquaintance, especially for those who live in a retired place, where they may hope to preserve their favourites from the fowler's snares, as well as from their own gardener's guns.

I cannot pretend here, however, to lay down unfailing rules ; I can only mention plans which I have practised, or heard of from those on whose testimony I can depend. The simple cottage plan of feeding the birds at the door-step in winter, when the snow is swept away, or on the window-sills when the bold applicants come at our breakfast-time to mention that they have none, are certainly very good beginnings of an *entente cordiale*.

Visiting nests is also useful. I made it so much a thing of course that I am not aware of any great precautions that need be taken : of course, one moves gently, and does not speak, except to the bird. In feeding the young it is better to begin on the third or fourth day, before they can see, as then they are used to one's voice, and to the way of feeding.

Stale bread, crumbled and scalded, the water poured off and a little cold milk poured on and beaten up, is, I think, the food that answers most gene-rally, serving for both hard and soft-billed birds. A little finely pounded yolk of egg is an improve-ment, if the birds do not seem to like it without. This preparation should be made fresh each time, and the milk must not be sour, nor the egg kept more than a few hours. A quill, the end cut round, and a little notch, two or three inches higher, for admitting air, is the best thing for feeding with, a very small piece being dropped into each of the widely gaping beaks. The food should be given neither quite cold nor at all hot.

2. Birds so trained to know one grow up pretty tame. I used to take them in and out of the nests ; and very often a young bird gets hurt, or a Swallow

tumbles down from its own nest, and it may be nursed
till it has come to be quite at home. I have brought
up many and many a Swallow, though, of course,
not for a cage.

In many cases a Swallow once tamed returns
again, year by year, to the well-known places, and
with many birds a friendship seems to be hereditary,
the young pairs becoming more and more familiar.
In another chapter I have alluded to birds brought
up from the nest, either in a cage fed by the parents,
or by hand ; and also to such as having been rescued
either from cold or from any accident have grown
quite tame ; these will hop about us, tap at the
window, come in at the door, call when they see us,
and be, in fact, the most amusing and bold of socially
disposed birds.

3. Even in London people can find some interest
in the Sparrow tribe. It may be remarked that the
pet cage-birds are mostly themselves of the sparrow
class ; but at any rate friendships are sometimes
struck up, which are truly amusing ; and the audacity
of the young Sparrow broods feeding within a yard
of me, and stealing the food put down for my own
birds, often affords me much entertainment : and
their attitudes, basking in the sun, or taking dust
baths, are very attractive while they are young and
pretty.

They come too on my windows, and have great

flirtations with some of my canaries—a noisy flirta-
tion it is, both parties rattling against the window-
pane—and great is my bird's excitement when she
hears her sparrow.

Sparrows, though plebeian, are good hearted birds.
I have heard of cases where they have continually
fed a cage bird, or a nest full of young hung outside
a window.   It is an experiment in the result of which
I have but little doubt, though my fondness for
feeding birds myself has deterred me from trying it.
In winter it is by no means rare to find a half-starved
bird, and as such a one is very likely to stay willingly
indoors while the cold weather lasts; by the time
that is over it is tolerably tame and accustomed to
its new home.

These winter-caught birds, I think, should always
be let out before the spring comes on.   If the cage
is then hung outside for a day or two and kept well
supplied with food, it will probably induce the bird
to keep up the acquaintance, and to return in any
trouble to the house that sheltered it.   These means
at any rate make the birds about a place tame and
fearless, and add tenfold to the pleasure of hearing
their pleasant songs.

4. As an instance of this pleasantest way of rearing
birds to be tame, I may quote the account which
Bishop Stanley gives of a Nightingale, a bird, it
must be remembered, of the shyest habits.   This

Nightingale was reared from the nest, and soon becoming tame it was kept in a cage till that May two
years, singing always in the winter from Christmas
till April, and showing no symptoms of impatience at
the usual time of migration ; it was silent the rest
of the year.   In that May it was permitted to go out
of its cage, which was hung up open at the door of
the offices. At first it returned regularly in the evening
to its cage, and was taken in, and released again the
next morning. As the season advanced, it sometimes
stayed out all night in the shrubberies and pleasure-
grounds, but if called by any one of the servants,
whose voice it knew, would return and feed out of
his hand. For a day or two, towards the close of
the summer, it seemed rather uneasy, but this soon
wore off. As the evenings got cool, in the autumn,
it returned to its cage before nightfall, and was taken
as usual into the house ; as the season still further
advanced it was permanently housed, and was expected
to sing again at Christmas.

CHAPTER XIII.

CAGES.

1. THE kinds of cages made are innumerable.
Amongst the great variety there is, it is surprising
that there are not many which are more desirable.

Cages are, however, more difficult to make good in all respects than might be expected; for, in many points, it is not easy to reconcile health, good appearance, convenience for cleaning, wholesomeness, and, often, we must add, economy of expense.

Paint and brass are hurtful; zinc cages and those with a large metal surface are extremely cold; common wooden ones are supposed to require painting, and to be hard to clean; while those of mahogany or any ornamental wood are a great deal more expensive. Glass cages again are high in price, and doubtful as regards their usefulness, the slightest chip being even more dangerous than a painted cage could be.

2. It has often struck me, what particularly good cages could be made of *papier mâché*. If bands and a tray of this were substituted for the zinc, and the food boxes and cans for the water glasses made in the same material, the birds would have the advantage of an extremely warm, comfortable cage, which could be quickly cleaned and dried, while its peculiar lightness would be a great advantage to those who have to lift it, and particularly in the case of hanging up a large cage.

I hope to get this idea carried into effect at some time; at any rate for the cages of the more tender birds, and for perches of every length, and in every sort of cage. Its usual colour is black, but this might suit well with the bird's bright plumage.

Baths also are often difficult, because of their weight, to manage. The use of *papier maché* would render them much lighter.

3. Most cages are defective, I find, as to their arrangements concerning seed and water. Little shallow tins, from which the seed is continually spilt; and water vessels, made to hang on outside in such a manner that the slightest movement may turn aside the mouth, and leave the poor little creatures within to die of thirst in the sight of water.

I do not think these glasses can be too much condemned. The mere injury the birds often get in striking against the rim deserves some little notice; and the danger of their not reaching the water is enough to make all who are fond of their birds unhappy, when unable themselves to see to them.

If they must be used, the only safety seems to me to be in having a small glass kept filled inside the cage as well, and that has many disadvantages.

The zinc cages have little barrels which turn round for filling; and these are much more suitable, though I do not think for cages anything is better than the old-fashioned drawers with holes made in them for the birds' heads to go through at the upper edge. For water, the self-supplying fountains, or the same covered drawers are also very fitting.

The mahogany breeding-cages are often faulty in these respects. Otherwise, when rather a close

cage is desirable, *if it ever is*, they might be serviceable.

4. I must not, however, pretend to speak as of
personal experience in many kinds of cages. Those
that I infinitely prefer to any are the commonest;
and though good materials and workmanship may
render them ornamental, my adherence to the plainest
prevents my knowing much of other kinds.

The glass cages made by Mr. Hawkins look bright
and gay. I believe their price is about two guineas
and a half, but I do not know how the birds thrive
in them. The slightest chip, where even the perches
are glass, is very dangerous, and I doubt whether
they can be warm enough. To the Zollverein cages
which I have tried I have a great dislike, for birds
in general. The quantity of metal seems to chill a
bird so thoroughly; thus letting alone the question,
not yet quite settled, as to the paint being hard
enough to resist all pecks, they do not seem to me
safe cages for any bird to be allowed to roost in.
Some of mine never do so without catching cold.
And as to the facilities of cleaning, I do not think
that properly-tended birds need meet with any difficulty in a plain wooden cage.

I do not know if it is true that the cage was in
fault, as it was not a thing I wished to experiment
on further; but some of my canaries in a zinc cage
suffered much from their feet, which seemed red and

painful. The cause was supposed to have been the
cold zinc floor they had been standing on. The
remedy—strewing the floor of another (a wooden)
cage, with oatmeal—soon restored their comfort.

It was the only time I knew them so troubled, and
the only time that they lived at all in a metal cage
during the winter months. When they are kept in
one, a thick, warm covering at night is absolutely
essential at all times, except, perhaps, in the very heat
of summer.

These cages are in some ways tempting ; they look
pretty, are quickly cleaned, and afford the birds a
great amount of light, which they think so much of.
At the same time a cage made of wood may be quite
as open, and does not *add* to the only fault of open-
ness the further chill of an extended surface of metal,
which is said to withdraw heat from an animal.

5. The square or oblong wooden cages, of which
I am so fond, are simple enough, not to say common
in their design and shape. The lowest usual form
is that of the regular market cages, made in stained
or painted deal, at about six shillings a dozen. That
size is six inches square, and is useful for a large
assemblage of scholars taking a music lesson.

Those cages, however, made of polished wood are
very cheap and useful, or it answers very well to
have them stained and varnished. Where use is the
thing needed, as in cages to hang up in an aviary,

I cannot too strongly advise the adoption of such patterns. If they are thought too cold, or require shading, a glass can be slid in, or a green baize curtain drawn over. They are very nice for standing in a window, made just to fit; a glass outside the front wire keeping in the seed and litter, if necessary, and the birds enjoying the full light in good view of their mistress. These cages are convenient when made eighteen inches high and wide, and exactly to fit the whole length of the window. One of four feet long, made in stained and varnished deal, would not exceed in price twelve shillings. In mahogany its cost would be about sixteen shillings, and if one end is glazed for a bath all round, the amusement of watching the birds will be great. A cage like this will hold quite two dozen birds.

6. Being so low priced, a second cage can probably be used, so that the two would be thoroughly washed by turns, and well dried and aired.

Any wood susceptible of polish could be employed. Maple looks well, but in boudoirs or drawing-rooms it would generally be better to let it match the furniture or the window-frame itself; whatever is the material, it must be solid, with no veneers or inlaying in any part that the birds can get at.

7. These cages can have an eating-room at one end, with the walls wholly or partly of glass outside the wire to keep the seed in, or they may be supplied

merely with the food-boxes elsewhere described as the best for all kinds of plain wooden cages. I think, however, the two shut-in apartments, one at each end, for food and bathing, is a good arrangement. A long, well-polished round perch should run along the front and back of the cage, the front next the room particularly, because if the birds are tame they will probably, when they want anything, come and sit in one long line along the front, looking at their mistress, and making their meaning generally quite clear to her.

8. Nothing adds so much to the birds' delight as well as to their beauty, as having a sort of shelf, about five inches wide, on which a box full of roses, myrtles, and other plants may stand, forming a hedge of foliage between them and the window.

Hanging baskets of plants near to the cage adds also much to its attractiveness, and the bath may be made the prettiest of room ornaments.

I have a cage of this kind that stands along a very large deep plant case, generally full of the gayest flowers, and it is very delightful in the morning to see the sun shining among the flowers, and the birds in a perfect tremble of song and happiness.

9. For very small and beautiful birds, such as the charming Waxbills, or Averdavatts, nothing does better than a cage of maple or of satin-wood, with little silvered wires. These birds are really worthy of a

pretty home, and their grains of millet are harmless ; they do not make any litter, and are pretty to stand upon a table. A bell-shaped cage, with a fairy rose-tree, or some very small plant in it, looks well ; a pot should be fitted into a wooden or gutta percha floor with a rim all round, and the bell-shaped cage would then drop down over it, fitting to the rim ; while the perches should rather *go through* the tree than over it.

10. A similar arrangement does charmingly for Wrens. They delight particularly in a little fir-tree, on which they can perch and hop up and down. They do best of all, however, in a finely-latticed enclosure of *wood* instead of wire (fine wicker almost like basket-work) ; and in winter the safest plan is to let them fly about the room and nestle into boxes filled with the softest moss.

I have never dared to let Master Bobby out at the same time as the Wrens, for Robins have a peculiar enmity to their own particular race ; and the story of Cock Robin and Jenny Wren has fixed in my mind too firmly the idea of their relationship for me to shake it off.

11. A Thrush, a Blackbird, or a pair of Doves should have a large square wicker cage. The Thrush is easily kept, and is a most delightful inhabitant of a garden. Hung up in a tree where he has air and sun, a little shade in the hot weather, and shelter in

the cold, he seems very happy, and sings—as only Thrushes do sing. Nothing is more delightful than to hear them in the early morning, and they sing nearly all the year.

Doves, too, require a large wicker cage open all round, in which they are very happy, and build—no, they certainly do not build much—for they deposit their eggs often on the bare nest basket. They lay, however, several times each year, and bring up two young each time, generally a pair. They require to have much air, but to come in doors at night.

12. If Larks are kept, they are seldom happy, but perhaps in a long high cage they may be least unhappy. A piece of strong net, or of some green material should be strained over the top, to prevent the poor bird from striking against the cage should he attempt to rise up and sing. The white linen advised by some writers, should never be used; and to be away from the fresh green fields, and from the blue clear air, is quite bad enough, without the further torture of a wall of whitewash to blind him with the glare. Larks soar without perching, so that perches are not wanted.

The more airy and open their cage can be the better. Two feet by eighteen inches is a good size, and the drawer for sand should be deep. Chaffinches also prefer rather long cages, the shape, for instance, of a double cube.

13. A family of Tom Tits and a pair of Water Wagtails, in a good-sized bell cage, are extremely amusing; but it should contain a large dish of water with a rock in the middle, which may support a tree or branch for perching on.

14. Breeding cages are best made of mahogany or some polished wood. They have generally two small square spaces intended for the nests, and a long division in which the little birds of the first brood might live. I think, however, it should never be used for this, as the young birds do better in a larger cage put so as to touch the other. To have one end, as well as the front, of wire, would be an immense advantage in these too gloomy cages. They are made with drawers too, which is a great mistake, as the jar and grating of removing them is injurious. I think the best plan is to have " a slide," that is, a slip of wood which pushes out and allows the sand within to be scraped out. Laying a couple of sheets of gutta percha, or even of stiff brown paper, on the floor all ready covered with a layer of sand, answers well in some ways; in that case, the upper one being drawn off, the lower one is left all clean. It is said, that a few drops of sweet oil dropped in the crevices of the cage, painted on with a feather, or dropped on paper, will effectually preserve the cage from any troublesome insects, which, if they ever come, are most to be feared just while the nest is there.

15. The little cheap square cages do as well as anything for a long line of school cages, and for hospital cages, which are very essential for wounded birds. A good plan is to take the wires entirely out of one about eight inches square, and to sew round the frame, at each corner, a tightly strained piece of canvas or flannel. I much prefer the latter. The top should be done in the same way, and a box or tray, arranged to contain food, sand, and water, should go along the door.

The floor does best covered thickly with bran, or even with coarse oatmeal, this being often cooling as well as soft ; everything of wool is objectionable, on account of the hairs which twist round the claws. All perches should always be moveable in this cage. If a bird's leg is wounded, no perch should be left in it ; but if it is the wing, one would be advisable. A water vessel, in which it could bathe if it wished, is much to be desired ; but it should be at the door, or hooked on, so as to cause no disturbance in filling or refilling. If a bird is rather sick than hurt, the same arrangements may still answer well, but warmth in this case is generally the principal thing needed, and the bird should be laid on a piece of flannel, and kept in a warm place, so that when there are many birds, at least two hospital cages of each kind are desirable in order to change the patient from the one to the other.

16. When also the English birds are sometimes bought very wild, or when the poor little Warblers are to be kept in autumn, cages lined with something soft may save pain. I mention it because, if it is to be done, it may as well be done gently ; but when a newly-bought bird beats wildly against the bars, or when a soft-billed bird in autumn dashes against its cage in the vain attempt to burst its wire prison, let those who keep it know that it is for its liberty it is almost dying.

Chapter XIV.

AVIARY CAGE.

1. In describing an aviary cage, I think it will bo well to record the fashion of one that was made for me when I was a very little child, and which lasted an immense time. During the time that it was in use, a few improvements were thought of, and these have been embodied in making the cage I now quote as a model. My original cage was of deal, being made at first as a mere experiment, and when found to answer we would not discard it. I, indeed, formed an opinion in favour of deal for bird cages, which has never been in the least relinquished, and in which the birds themselves certainly bear me out.

The inside of this cage was not painted at all, though the outside was thoroughly, as it used in summer to stand out of doors. The top of this cage had a sloping roof, from which the rain ran off, and a waterproof curtain used to be hung up at night before the wire front.

The two sides being separated by a wire grating, the young birds were often kept in one division, with, perhaps, a party of a different kind overhead, their own parents still being kind to them through the dividing bars.

In the winter, the partitions being opened, the whole number, sixteen or twenty, would live together happily.

2. One very good plan to adopt in having this kind of cage, is to have one half made permanently separated by a wire division from the other, while that other is so arranged, by means of brackets, serving for perches when not in use, as to support the floor of an upper story not more than a foot from the top, or at different heights going up.

The advantage of this plan is that the two sides can contain couples which would be disposed to molest each other in their building, while the small division up-stairs, when the cage is in three compartments, forms a roomy nursery for any broods of young birds that may require a little feeding after they have left their mother. If a perch or branch is placed near the wires, the old bird will very often patronise his children, and example is of great service in teaching them to wash and make themselves look respectable.

This is of such consequence, that when my young birds (bought when just fledged) do not do well in this way, I put a very dandy bird, either Chaffie or Goldie, in the adjoining part, that by seeing him they may be fairly shamed by the elaborateness of his toilette.

Many people divide *lengthways* an aviary like this; some, again, contrive a third story in winter, at least, by removing the front slope of the roof and substituting wire. The top should, however, have a ceiling when out of doors for protection from heat and damp in the summer time, and from cold in winter.

I myself prefer very much the high divisions, as the birds seem fond of hopping up and down; they admit also a much nicer tree, and show the inmates off to greater advantage.

3. No paint, I need hardly say, should be used inside, and no brass whatever.

If glass is adopted, the maker must be particularly warned to put the putty entirely outside.

I do not think any wood really answers better than well smoothed and polished deal; but many persons dislike it, and it is merely a fancy perhaps of my own, though having seen how well it has answered, I have now a preference for it. Mahogany is particularly unsuitable to display the birds' bright plumage.

4. Where it is desired to keep Canaries separate
from English birds, two divisions answer extremely
well ; and if the top of the cage is made flat in the
centre, or to rise to a shelf at the back, single cages
can stand all along it, containing one or two especial
birds or singers : and as it is with Canaries a law of
the Medes and Persians to allow no singing over their
own heads (if they can put it down), all those who
are underneath will warble indefatigably. A good
party of English birds, Linnets, Redpoles, Chaffinches,
Goldfinches and Siskins, are delightful to have in such
a cage. A single Bullfinch I should recommend to
be kept overhead ; and if valuable foreign birds form
part of the collection, I should advise either a third
central division for them, making the whole thing
larger, and covering their partitions carefully with
green baize in cold weather, at least at night, or else
the Canaries might be put in with the other finches,
trusting to their agreeing.

At any rate they can be very happy, and if it is
difficult to bring up a young family well there, an
attached couple can always be disposed of in another
case while they are employed in rearing their young.
One way of managing would be to have only hen
Canaries in the English aviary, and as they are
extremely pretty, the cock birds must either be contented to sing outside, or build, with well-chosen mates,
in separate cages. Sometimes, however, they disgrace

themselves by terribly low matches, and then they must run the chance of being ousted from their nest; the skirmish only adding to the amusement of the aviary.

5. The English wild birds do not often build together in cages unless they have been brought up in the same place from the nest, for though they may build, the instinct of hiding her nest and eggs, while sitting, is often too strong for the hen bird to get over. The best chance is to pretend you do not see her (not to let her *see* you see her), unless she is very tame. Canaries, on the contrary, often do not care a straw; mine eat biscuit in their nest when I hold it within reach, and seem obliged to me for thus enlivening their solitude. Of course, when no divisions are wanted, only one large space, matters are greatly simplified.

A very good way, then, is to have the whole front wire-work unbroken, as well as the back, which may be of wood or glass; the tray would then draw out at one end, and the feeding apparatus fit in at the same.

It is by no means a bad plan to have separate little dining and bath rooms in such an establishment, the same as I mentioned in speaking of the long, narrow cage.

6. Another good arrangement is to have at one end a small trough or box, in which some shrubs sunk in

pots are growing ; the tray then runs close up to this box, leaving also untouched a slip at the other side, on which stand the bathing and eating houses. But perhaps the easiest and pleasantest plan of all is to have at each end a trough sunk in the floor, and filled with plants, cress and lettuce growing about the roots. The centre should contain one large fir or myrtle growing in a rough box or flower-pot, and the tray in two parts should draw out by the glass lifting up at the back. The bath would then be under the tree at one side, while the dining-rooms would be drawers with holes, or little square glass houses placed in each corner.

This aviary would look excessively pretty, and from the thorough opening it would allow at the back, each separate part could be kept as clean as possible.

When glass is used, the birds soon understand that they must not knock against it, though frights in this case are dangerous. In an aviary of this kind nothing can be prettier than to watch the birds sitting upon the trees, and playing in the bath.

Perches, rounded and polished, should fit into niches or against the wires, going all along the cage, as well as one rather near the front wire, and also one at the back. For containing the seed, boxes about two inches wide and deep are the best I know. There seems great room for improvement in most cages in

this respect, as in open trays the birds waste their
seed terribly, while if they can get into it, it is both
scattered about and spoilt.

Small round holes in front, and wire gauze over
the top, prevent this great waste of seed, and though
a long row of apparent mouse-trap holes does not
look very pretty, this is much the best for the birds,
as the wire causes many sharp, painful blows to their
eager little bills, which are by no means so insensible
as often is supposed to the jars they get. In this
respect I think the more we return to the old-fashioned
drawers and holes the better for the birds ; and the
great objection that used to exist to these—the
difficulty in thoroughly cleaning wood—may be
readily overcome.

I am much in favour of a double set of food-holders,
changing them each day, so as to ensure a good
washing, drying, and airing. And for the inside, it
is most desirable to have a glass or carthenware
lining. When several are required, or when one
maker is fitting up many cages, it may be worth
while having their drawers made on purpose : otherwise, I have found the glass or china trays used for
holding pens answer very well for this, and the deeper
they are the better. One of these for the seed, and
another for the drinking water, would answer very
well, the deepest being for water ; and if the drawer
is rather longer than these two divisions, it is no

bad plan to fill the space with a mixture of old lime, red sand, and chalk, which will be very useful in keeping the birds in health. The boxes should be so arranged as to be got at easily by doors, as the water should be changed twice a day in summer; the seed sifted and refilled daily, and the filling-up mixture every now and then.

7. I will conclude this chapter by giving the exact working description of an aviary cage I have lately had made by the pattern, in great measure, of that before alluded to. Mine has been made in a tolerably satisfactory manner by J. Millar, Cotter's Place, Old Brompton. This cage painted and varnished would cost about five pounds. Woodwork entirely, of well seasoned deal. Wire-work, *tin*, (on many accounts to be much preferred.) Dimensions: height, from floor to top, four feet, *i.e.* from floor to spring of slope, three feet, and one foot allowed for the slope of the roof. Width, two feet; length, four feet. The top slopes down from a shelf six inches wide, which is at the back. The whole front, back, sides, and top, are of the tin wire mentioned. The bottom has a drawer made in two parts to draw out, and a wire partition runs up the cage, and is unhooked at pleasure. A green baize curtain can be drawn round the cage, and a floor (a tray itself) can be put in to divide each side into two stories—making four in all. The doors are all at the ends, which also open entirely. The

seed boxes are made covered, and have drawers lined with glass for containing the seed and water. They stand in the cage, and have small perches fastened to them, which look very pretty when crowded with birds.

8. The great charm of this cage is, that standing in a window the birds have full air and light, while perfectly visible from within and without. In the summer, therefore, they can stand entirely outside, and the cage being light is easily supported. When nicely arranged, fronted with a few plants and creepers, and with a bath, &c., it is extremely pretty, and the birds' bright plumage makes it look almost as gay as flowers, even in the gloomier time of year when only evergreens can make up " a wood."

<hr>

CHAPTER XV.

THE ROOM AVIARY.

1. I BELIEVE one of the least troublesome and most enjoyable of aviaries is that fitted up in a small spare room—a breakfast-room, for instance. To do this properly is very little trouble. It is better to take the paper off the walls, but not essential; then the walls themselves may be simply plastered;—the birds will certainly peck the plaster, but it only does them good to do so.

2. The glass sashes have to be covered with wire-work, or are, some say, much better taken out altogether during the summer months. I do not quite agree to that view myself, as it seems to me that the means of closing a window is not to be despised in case of heavy storms ; and, putting aside the birds, I have visions of housemaids in confusion, and of footmen in dismay when "the water has come through." Besides a permanent open window-frame does not tend to warm, in spring and autumn, the adjoining rooms. Thus I should be much disposed, with all due deference to those who advocate the more open plan, to advise that the window-sashes should be left in place, covered within with a frame in which wire-work has been fitted, the top sash being let down every day in spring and autumn, and in summer both day and night. A Venetian blind outside, or between the window and the wire, is a great gain if the room looks south, and the windows can then always be closed directly if any violent storm comes on.

3. I have known birds often die in numbers a few days or hours after a severe thunder-storm, to the glare and fear of which the poor frightened things had been exposed. When any such alarming event is going on, I always let in my birds to my own room, and talk to, and pet them, which is an evident consolation, for no one knows how much they get

to consider human beings as made entirely for their own special use and comfort. While I write these words one creature in yellow is pecking seeds from off my very paper!

4. For the floor of the room it is very advisable to have oil-cloth, which can now and then be taken up to be cleaned, and which can also be frequently washed. I do not know that this is indispensable, but it certainly prevents any accumulation of sand in the joints of a boarded floor.

5. There should be here again some grove contrivance, and a row of trees in large flower-pots round the room is far the best and prettiest. I recommend spruce firs, one on each side the window, and one or two more in each corner. The privet and box are also good shrubs for the purpose, as the birds do not eat their leaves, which is more than one can say of most plants. And the outside of the window is the place of all others for a hanging garden.

For any one living in the country, perhaps large branches of fir and gorse are best, and most convenient, as they can be got so easily in spring, the fir being cut in March, before the sap begins to flow; this preserves its leaves and looks anything but ill.

These should be fastened up, by means of two or three little blocks of wood nailed to the wall, or rising from the skirting-board, and a long horizontal bar screwed to them, leaving only just room to stick in the branches between it and the wall. This plan too has, no doubt, been found to answer well, as it is given by Mr. Brent in the *Cottage Gardener*, the instructions in which I always find work well.

My own fashion for any kind of aviary is trees. because, living in London, I like at least to make believe a wood; and it is pleasant to feel that in a "bird's-eye view" it may even be deemed a forest.

6. Having a room like this affords great opportunities of taming and playing with the birds: while for those who have a weakness for "keeping things in their proper places," a glass door into the next room gives a pretty view of the various antics played while keeping the birds quite separate.

7. In such a room, however, we must beware of mice; they utterly spoil any food they touch for the birds that have to eat it; indeed, I believe it is even made very injurious by them: and as people cannot actually keep both cats and birds—unless the cat is a genius, like one of ours, who knew that the birds were "friends," and let them perch upon him, and even peck his ears—great care is needed to guard against such inroads.

8. At building time, too, one must keep a strict look-out amongst the birds themselves, watching them when they are going on as usual, not when just flurried by the entrance of some one into their abode,

unless, indeed, they are so tame as to go on with their squabbles, and make no difference for the presence of a visitor.

I think, when all are paired, or mostly so, they generally keep themselves to themselves in a pretty contented manner, but sometimes there seems, for some unexplained cause, to be a general prejudice against some unhappy little couple, and their nest gets pulled to pieces and they themselves are grievously maltreated by many of the others joining in the attack.

In such cases, a common breeding cage is useful, with some slight contrivance to protect the nest, if built, as it sometimes is, against the outer wires : but a good deal of vigilance is needed, as I said, in listening for the sounds of battle—that peculiar sharp hissing—and in observing if many feathers are strewed about, a wing or tail feather, especially, betraying that there has been a scuffle.

9. It is as well also to remark that when birds are hungry they invariably take to fighting, for which reason the seed boxes, standing upon the floor, or fixed against the walls, should never become quite empty.

10. We must not forget the kitchen garden, having at present provided only for the trees. It is aggravating to grand gardeners, perhaps, to be requested to send one up a small parcel of groundsel seed,

chickweed cuttings, and water-cress roots, with an injunction also on *no* account to forget the thistle seed and dandelions; but these delicacies greatly delight the dickies. A set of shallow garden pans standing in some out of the way corner, are good things to have for this food, and turfs with a hole scooped out in them are also capital pans.

11. Birds are so very fond of seeing anything moving, that there should be a vine trained about their windows, the branches waving outside, and the flickering shadow will delight them much. Swings are also valuable playthings. I like to have them all round, here and there, especially so placed as to show the birds against a background of green leaves. They also look well on a level with hanging flower baskets, which are great ornaments in, or rather outside, an aviary, the framing carried across a little way out, from one corner post to the other along the front, being just the thing on which to hang them.

The higher the side rows of trees, and the lower the front one of plants, the better pleased will be the inhabitants of the place; who are as fond as can be of gay colours and pretty, cheerful-looking homes.

12. Perhaps, a window facing the east may be in some respects the best aspect for the birds, being early risers, as they are proverbially; but I prefer

myself a west window for them; as a south look-out is so much too hot in summer, and at the west they get, after all, the softest and least keen winds. When they can see a cheerful stream of sunshine in front, or on one side, or when they are such spoiled little Dickies as to be let come in to breakfast with their mistress, sunning themselves then in an eastern window, I do not think they will be likely to complain very loudly. I ought here to remark, for the benefit of those who are perplexed as to their own room's open windows, that Hay-ward's hexagon netting, or a panel of some woollen material, as green baize, damped and put up, will both keep the room cool in summer, and provide against a sudden elopement of the little visitors.

The great amusement of the day is the bath, however, both to birds and mistress, but this will be described hereafter.

13. Any separate cage hung in such a room should always (if secure against the intrusion of cats and mice) be hung rather low. Of course the light even from the largest window is much less full close to the ceiling than it is low down, and this both birds and plants find often to their cost.

In cold nights, however, the higher the better for the birds to roost, as draughts and sudden changes of temperature are about the very worst things that they can undergo.

CHAPTER XVI.

OUT-DOOR AVIARY, AND BIRDS FOR IT.

1. A REALLY well-formed aviary appears to me to be very rarely met with. There is one mentioned by Mr. Shirley Hibbert, which must be very charming; a large conservatory looking towards the east, being duly wired, and provided with the sloping bank of plants and turf, and the fragrant flowers in which birds delight.

This is, however, a thing far beyond the unassisted management of an amateur, and is probably kept in order at a great expense.

My own experience in regularly built out-door aviaries is extremely limited; in fact, I never had one of those in my own care at all. Those I have known have been either mere large portable enclosures, or an end of a greenhouse wired off, or a room in the house adapted for the purpose; the first and last plans being those I have adopted myself.

Mr. Kidd, the story of whose aviary of nearly four hundred birds is very widely known, does not allow the possibility of letting birds in aviaries have the opportunity of mateing among themselves, and bringing up young families. He seems to consider the birds as only kept for song, and for their pleasant company; and in the view of preserving peace, he would forbid the admittance of any ladies to the large society.

Of course this is quite a question of taste, but certainly many persons would think that no amount of song would compensate for losing the variety, and for missing the pretty sight of the little fledglings, being also deprived of the amusement of witnessing the courtships. It is so diverting to see the birds singing for the approbation of some very much sought for lady, who sits meanwhile with her head on one side, sometimes deigning to listen, but always pretending *not* to see the gentleman she prefers.

Canaries are said to choose their mates by song; that is to say, the finest singer has generally first choice of a wife; thus even for singing I cannot imagine an aviary being improved by the absence of all these competitions, and all variety would be lost.

2. Mr. Kidd, it seems, did *wish* his birds to build, and I cannot help thinking that their failure to bring up their young was naturally to be attributed to the immense crowd they lived in; besides the nest boxes were nailed, so Mr. Kidd implies, upon the wall, and thus the idle birds had full access to them. Had the numbers of the aviary been a little more within bounds, or had a thick hedge been arranged all round the wall for dodging about and hiding it, I cannot fancy the difficulty half so great; and even at the worst, a good flight of canary hens would probably

9—2

have succeeded. It is certainly always *doubtful* if Canaries and other hen Finches will agree to live peaceably ; still it does answer sometimes, *when they are put into the aviary in established pairs*, the couples generally being faithful to each other, and each being occupied in its own important work, just, in fact, as if they were out of doors. If, therefore, any very large bird is from the first excluded during the building season, very naughty or mischievous small birds imprisoned, and only pairs of birds admitted, or a number of Canary hens (or of home-bred Linnets, which answer charmingly), the peace of the aviary will be in the main preserved, and a great attraction and interest added to it during the summer months. It must be understood, however, that it should be Canaries *or* Linnets, not both together, if put in in numbers ; or in a divided aviary, Canaries on one side, and Linnets and Goldfinches and other hens with their respectives mates on the other, would be very pretty.

Any particular pair of any sort could be enclosed in a breeding-cage, and it is well to have a few empty cages of this kind standing open in case birds formerly used to them may wish to build again in them. But now, in proceeding to give a few hints for the formation of large aviaries, I shall take it for granted that it is an object that the birds should breed ; and as I have been very careful to gain all the information possible from others, I hope that my not having possessed exactly such an aviary myself may not prevent the directions being well founded, as far as concerns the birds and their requirements.

3. As interesting a fixed aviary as any I have known, is formed from one end of a moderate sized conservatory. The space, about twelve feet wide, was merely wired off with galvanized zinc wire, the surrounding glass being also lined with wire. The birds here gain the morning sun, but in winter, when it is very cold, the glass walls are screened from without by shutters.

The birds in such a position are very warmly housed, and the sweet scent of the flowers adds greatly to their pleasure. In the enclosed space, which is rather narrow, a row of evergreen shrubs is placed along the back, and grouped closely at each corner, the higher trees nearly reaching the top; and again in the centre, three or four more are grouped. In an aviary like this, it has a charming effect when a pretty bath is suspended from the roof in one of the wire baskets; by the use of some strong cement the outside may be made pretty, ornamented with shells and coral, like the plaything that it is; and there the birds will amuse themselves for hours, pretending to be frightened, and putting in one foot and pulling it out again, behaving for all the world just like naughty children. The seed and water-troughs recommended in the chapter referring to them are all that is required in the way of furniture; they should be fixed against the side walls, a little door giving ready access to them. The floor being formed of tiles or stone, and the walls also being solid, there is every reason to hope that further precautions against mice and rats will be quite unnecessary. Their presence certainly should be guarded against with every care imaginable. If in an aviary of this kind a group of firs—especially the spruce firs—are gathered in each corner, with one or two oranges and myrtles in the centre, there will be fair hiding-places, and it may be hoped that the birds will build.

4. Keeping here a dozen English Finches, Linnets, and Siskins, with a dozen pair of Canaries, and a dozen Canary hens, the probabilities are that the morning melody will be gay enough. A pair of Nightingales, not more than one (as they are jealous birds, and the worst singer gets sulky), one or two Blackcaps, some Willow Wrens and Garden Warblers, with perhaps a Woodlark, would make a very delightful concert. Even the Nightingales will sometimes build in a quiet aviary; and in a division made against the house wall, especially if slightly shaded by climbing plants, it is very likely they might be induced to do so.

The Wrens also may, if they are very tame, build in an ivied wall in such an aviary, and a lovely little structure indeed the Wren's nest is; so deep and soft, with ten or twelve little pinkish eggs about the size of peas, and the chicks when they appear are so deeply buried in their soft bed of down, that although I have found their nests very early in the spring—once, I think, before February was half through—they always seemed to be cuddled in warmly and snugly enough, under their little mamma's brown wings.

Larks sometimes will breed, it is said, in aviaries, but this I cannot answer for, not having ever tried them; but at any rate it seems as if they might be less unhappy than one would have feared.

Should divisions be wished for, a family of Tom Tits, provided with a tree, on the branches of which to hang, are the funniest and most impudent of pickles. Their impish ways are such, that it is hardly safe to admit them amongst others. But even in a large bell-cage they may display their ingenuity much to the amusement of those who like to see how naughty birds *can* be; or, though that is a little wicked, they may be suffered to persecute a Thrush.

5. If a floor has to be made, a very good plan is that recommended in the *Cottage Gardener* for making concrete walks. "A layer of stones, brickbats, shells, or clinkers, six inches deep; a layer of chalk or lime, in the proportion of one to ten of the stones or other foundation, well rolled, beaten and watered to the thickness of three inches,"—(for a floor it is

better to omit the directed rise of *two inches in the middle*, and substitute for it the same rule applied to a slight slope from the back to the front);—" over this lay half an inch of gravel and lime or fine chalk ; water, and roll well again." We may, or may not go on to add one eighth of an inch of the best coloured gravel, and again to roll until it is quite solid. The lime and gravel is, however, about the best thing birds can have to peck at.

6. It is another good plan, as I have already hinted, to have two sets of trees, and to turn out one row at a time to get the benefit of a few showers, whenever there are no nests actually in progress in their branches; always remembering, however, that the last shower had better be an artificial one, as London rain has not the most cleansing qualities. These trees require a good deal of water always, at any rate at the roots—and the thicker they stand together, the better the birds will like it when they are looking out for an attractive spot for nests.

The floor should be covered at least four inches deep with sand, and I think the best way is then to clean it out occasionally from the outside with a thing like a hoe, having first removed the plant shelf to render it accessible. The plant shelf, I ought to have said before, should be in fact a deep box along the front wall, filled nearly full of pieces of broken charcoal, with the top only covered with sand, and a layer of green moss in which the pots should stand. The perches, round and polished, should be made to fit in along the wire front, and near the ceiling. A flat panelled ceiling should be *always* used. A frame filled with felt and covered with waterproof cloth would answer well.

Along the front of such an enclosure, a few creepers trained on wires are beautiful—the blue Passion-flower, for instance, and the Japan honeysuckle. Hanging baskets of flowers also look very charming, while the gay yellow plumage, red bills, and crimson heads, of the bright inhabitants take the place of flowers within, and adorn the evergreens with the gayest balls of colour.

CHAPTER XVII.

BATHS, FOODHOLDERS, ETC.

1. WHAT pretty pebbles we can all remember gathering on the shore—so shining and so transparent! we quite thought cutting and polishing would be all unnecessary, and that our finds were gems. Alas! the pebbles got dry, and they were gems no longer; the lapidary looked contemptuous, and said they "were common flints," and we went home disconsolate. But now, I, for one, often wish that I had

those stones; common though they might be when dry, they looked very pretty wet, and in a bird-bath they have a chance of being so pretty often. If, then, any of my readers wish for an amusing work, they will pick up some pebbles and any shells they can; bits of spar, fossils, agate, jasper, cornelian, and all the rest, and with these they will build up the most charming baths.

This, I am certain, will be a great delight, at any rate to children, for it is pleasant to find a use for things that are so pretty, and that remind us pleasantly of some seaside holiday. On the Welsh coast, and in Cornwall, many of these treasures are easily to be found; and even inland places often afford us charming pieces of quartz or spar, or bits of limestone, thickly strewn with beautiful fossil shells.

The objection to grotto-building is, that it is of no use, and not ornamental either; but these baths are useful, and may be very pretty, and if all the grotto-builders now turn their minds to bird-baths, many a bird will return them grateful thanks.

2. Birds like always to have a good depth of water; at the same time, of course, they do not wish to be drowned. Their greatest delight, then, is to sit on a stone and bathe. I had last winter a pair of Goldfinches that regularly every morning bathed in a small aquarium, standing on the top of the piece of rock; they bent down their heads, and dashed the

water briskly all over their wings and plumage. Nice wet work it was, and in self-defence, a different bath, such as the birds might prefer, to this, really became essential. I have accordingly adopted a perfectly new arrangement, which to my idea is perfection, because the birds like it and can be seen enjoying it without the slightest hindrance, and without the discomfort of our being splashed all over.

3. One of the smallest glass milk pans is therefore prepared for bathing in. This can be easily hung up in a wire basket, like those used for flowers, in the front of an aviary, where a little splashing is likely to do no harm; but when the birds are in a room in a large cage, or flying loose about, I have a sort of glass house in which the bath can stand. A plant case answers admirably, when birds can be trusted in one, as Robins can, and three or four of the very smallest fish look pretty in them.

I will proceed, however, to describe how the bath is made, and afterwards it will be easy to fix on where to place it.

The glass milk pans sold by Millington, in Bishops-gate-street, are the best things I know for the forma-tion of such baths. They are made six, ten, fourteen inches in diameter—the sizes increasing up to twenty-six; the prices varying with the size, from sixpence to five and sixpence. These pans are much superior to hyacinth dishes, being of an infinitely better shape,

and a very much prettier make. The glass is slightly
green, but this only adds to the pleasing appearance.

4. These pans are very sloping, deepest in the
middle; and sometimes therefore a very large shell or
two look well in the centre fixed at the back together,
and with a number of little shells gathered about the
edge, with pretty bits of coral. For my own part, I
always like a bath to have some sand in it; it adds
much to the bather's comfort, as birds slip about upon
glass so much, and there can be no doubt that sand is
more natural. If, however, marine sand, shells, or
corals, are used, they cannot be too well washed first,
as salt water is hurtful. This need not imply any
excessive care, merely a good soaking for four and
twenty hours.

There may be a difficulty sometimes as to cement,
because the putty used in glazing is dangerous, as it
contains white lead; while in the case of any square
bath being used, some means are essential for fixing
the panes of glass together.

In his directions for aquariums, Mr. Shirley Hibberd
recommends Scott's cement, which is obtained from
Mr. Scott of Newcastle ; and as this can be conveyed
by post, it will probably be a useful hint to many persons not living in easy reach of places where such
things are sold.

The rockwork ought not to be fixed to the glass
itself. It is well to put it together in it, for the sake

of keeping exactly to the shape, but it should always be able to be taken in and out for cleaning. A pile in the middle, or a ring round the edge, is pretty, and easily arranged. Another very good plan is to take a small piece of zinc, about six inches in diameter, and spreading its surface with the Roman or Portland cement used in aquariums, to place in the middle one high jagged piece of rock. This piece being firmly fixed as a centre, little pieces of spar and crystal and stalactite may be piled up all round, and also fixed together by the bed of cement heaped around the base. Lava, polished fossils, and specimens of jasper and malachite also look well, mixed up in the heap. Then there may be some shells—those beautifully coloured harps, for instance, and the great ones lined with mother of pearl. The little creatures look so very pretty, balancing themselves on the edge, dashing down their heads, and fluttering their bright, transparent wings in the water in an ecstasy of delight!

5. The zinc foundation is of course to be hidden, and all to lift out together; it can thus be easily cleansed while wet, by water being allowed to pour down upon it, and during this process the vase can be also emptied. A flexible gutta percha tube attached to a little plug-hole does best for this, or an aquarium syringe will be found very useful, and the vase being emptied, the rock work may be replaced, and the whole

refilled with water, making it quite respectable for
our little friends to wash in.

6. They rush in sometimes four or five together, to
splash in the clean water like a little shoal of fishes.
They go paddling about, lifting up their feet very high
for each step, and making so much noise in setting them
down again, that any one would fancy that they were
web-footed, and holding up their tails so carefully out
of the water, like so many Jenny Wrens, as if to be
draggle-tailed was ignominious among birds ; sitting
at the water's edge shaking ; shaking so quickly that
one cannot see how they do it ; and then hopping in
again : and they will go in the same way each time.
I watched one the other day ; she took ten dips after I
began counting ; and each time she flew to one particular spot about three or four steps off, and took the
same series of short stages before she hopped in finally.
Sometimes a number bathe at the same time ; and
sometimes timid ones stand at the edge and let the
others splash them, and call that washing ; and then
again they wait and go in by turns. I hardly know
which way is most amusing. One day when the bath
was shallow I saw one bird lie down in it and turn over
to bathe the other side when the first was done ; that
was a brown Linnet, and brown Linnets certainly do
delight in water.

7. I can hardly venture to recommend so bold a
plan ; but I let my own birds bathe when they like in

winter. They have never suffered from it; and a
bird dealer and doctor whom I consulted said that he
believed a bird always could be trusted to go by its
own instinct, and so I think they can. If they are ill,
too, a bath seems to be their most universal remedy.
A bird looks mopy, and then ensues a grand bathing;
I observe a hearty luncheon follows, and the patient
brushes up and returns into active life. I may also
remark, that if a newly bought or unhappy bird can be
induced to bathe, it is the best of signs that it is
getting better.

8. A most excellent plan for this room bath is to have
a common square bird-cage, glazed, the floor being
covered with sand, and a bath, such as I have described, being then placed within it; we have thus the
full amusement without the slightest inconvenience.
Two or three little plants, such as ferns, may grow at
the corners, and fish may swim about in it. A
sliding side of glass makes the door of entrance as
large or small as necessary.

Where large baths are not required, a little japanned
tin one may be had, from ninepence upwards, for
hooking upon the cage door. Little square cages, too,
with the perches removed, and a china or glass dish put
in, make capital bath cages, and give the birds room to
splutter. They may be very easily glazed outside the
wires, to prevent too much splashing.

9. Perhaps the prettiest methods of all are imbedding

it in the moss and ferns of a plant-case, hanging it
in a wire frame surrounded with moss, in a greenhouse
or room aviary, or letting it stand on a moss-covered
pedestal.   In a cage, most probably, it would require
to hang near the floor, or to stand on it ; if there are
shrubs, it looks very pretty in the moss beneath them.

I hope, in what has been said on this subject,
nothing will have seemed to advocate a heap of trum-
pery and unmeaning ornaments.   My excuse for
introducing the subject so prominently as this is, that
some "heap of stones" or shells being required for
actual use, it seems absurd to avoid using a class of
objects which have been only rendered ridiculous by
being employed in things that are both ugly and
unmeaning.   The gathering of the materials, shells,
&c., is also a great delight, and if they could be
made useful it would add to the pleasure.

10. There is hardly anything in which modern
cages are more faulty than the seed and water vessels.
When I was a child, I had a number of old cages
that had been laid aside for I dare say ten years,
and, certainly, those cages were preferable to any that
I see now.   They had, I remember, things like wash-
hand-stands, which turned in and out, were fitted
with nice large glasses, and had a sort of roof to
prevent the birds walking into them.   The drawers,
too, were good deep ones, with a long row of holes for
the birds to eat through.

11. The horrible invention of hanging glasses has doubtless killed many birds, and even, without dying, to endure great thirst is the extremest suffering. For my own part, I cannot bear that my birds should run the risks which have been already adverted to in Chapter XIII.

The zinc cages have little turning cylinders (which clever birds walk out through), and these being fitted with tin seed-holders, the seed is upset directly; if they have glasses, the birds, at least young ones, very often hurt themselves against them. The little tin trays in breeding cages, with the outside glasses, seem to combine all the disadvantages possible to collect.

In Edinburgh, a kind of cage-fountain is or was much used, made of plain cut glass, with a well polished edge, and presenting to the bird a constant supply of water inside the cage. There is, also, a kind of barrel seed-box, through a hole in the side of which the bird obtains its food. The best plan, however, that I know of, suited to any good-sized cage or aviary, is a box, made with a sloping top and a deep drawer belonging to it, which should be lined with glass or earthenware; a row of round holes goes all along just above the drawer, and either a similar vessel is arranged for water, or a division in each separates the part for the seed from that which contains the water. A low perch goes along it, on which the birds sit when eating. The whole affair, woodwork as well as

10

glass, should, however, now and then, be cleaned out thoroughly. Tin or zinc is objectionable either for water or any kind of food. The pans for all kinds of paste, or egg, &c., should be of glass or earthenware. Terra cotta is a nice material to use in aviaries, not only for the food, but for the fountain, the flooring, and the plant boxes.

12. A white marble fountain is the most perfect thing, and when this is arranged with a small jet of water like the small Eau de Cologne fountains, the effect is charming when the gay plumaged birds keep diving through the spray.

13. The perches should always, in cages and in aviaries of all sorts, be made to take in and out ; and whether they are fixed or moveable, it is necessary to be careful that the birds do not catch their feet in any kind of cranny. Polished deal or maple is the best material, perhaps, after *cane* for this, but cane is at once a natural round perch for the bird's foot to grasp, perfectly light, and easy to be cleaned. Deal I am fond of myself, but this is merely because my birds have done well with it ; many other soft woods may be quite as good. Still, deal is quickly cleaned, and not at all apt to crack, which is much in its favour.

The perches should be kept perfectly clean ; and after washing with yellow soap and water, they should never be returned to the cage or aviary till quite dry. They should not, however, be dried too quickly, as that would warp them. In the cage they should be carefully arranged not to be just over each other. A good plan is to have one the whole way along both front and back; another higher up, farther into the cage, and another quite near the top. The birds like the high perches best, and the higher they roost the better on all accounts. Another advisable plan is to put the perches across the cage alternately in three stories; or to have the two long ones by the wires, and all the short ones crossing the other way. In the bell cages and so on, one perch should go from the seed to the water place, and then the other higher up, also across the cage.

Chapter XVIII.

LISTS OF BIRDS, AND WANTS OF BIRD-KEEPERS.

1. As I have often been withheld from ordering birds under the idea that they were much more costly than they really prove, I subjoin a list of a few of the prettiest birds I can find, naming, for the reader's guidance, the prices that I have given for them. In a few instances, I have not had the birds in my own possession, but the information is reliable, and the specimens appeared to be very good representatives of their respective kinds.

I do not myself find any particular difficulty in keeping foreign birds. In gardening it is much easier to grow exotic plants to something like perfection, than to keep in good health our little hedgerow flowers ; and with birds I fancy it is much the same, the temperature of our rooms suiting best those of a warmer climate.

Amongst the many kinds of pretty foreign birds I know nothing prettier for a work-table or stand than a small bell cage full of the beautiful Avadavats. They are very small birds, smaller than a Wren, and with their bright red beaks, spreading, fan-like tails, and exquisitely spotted plumage, are really lovely.

They sit in a line on their perch, singing, such a song as it is, continually ; being generally affectionate, but quarrelling at night for the inside place.

2. The wire of the cage for very small birds like these should be very fine, mine is only of tin ; but such birds as these are worthy of a silver or of a plated-wire dwelling ; there would be some advantage also in giving them such homes in showing their pretty movements. Brass must not be used ; and zinc is too cold ; while the colour of gilding is not nearly so becoming as that of silver.

3. In buying delicate foreign birds, I must strongly advise all purchasers to have the birds sent to their home by the dealer ; he perfectly understands how to deliver the bird in the safest manner and in the best

condition, while a lady putting a small birdcage into her carriage, and driving off with it for a round of shopping, is not unlikely to find her bird come to grief.

This is the safest plan ; at the same time I do not mean to say that birds cannot travel; I have had many from all parts of the country, and the first pair I ever possessed, two pretty Canaries, travelled down in a small wicker cage by railway, chaperoned by the guard, from London. The distance was one hundred and thirty miles, the last part of which was performed in the carrier's cart. But to return to the bird list.

4. The AVADAVATS are little brown and red spotted birds, with reddish backs and spreading tails, white feet, red beaks like sealing-wax, shrill, silvery, short song, and peculiarly graceful movements. They may be made very tame, and look exquisitely pretty in a company of birds of their own stature, Wrens, for instance, and little Silver Beaks, in a small enclosure, where, if there is some evergreen, they will dart about pluming themselves noisily, washing, and singing, and making the gayest of pictures. The other birds of the size suitable to live with the pets I mentioned, are Australian, African, St. Helena, Orange, and the exquisite Zebra Wax-bills ; all these are to be had at from twelve to fifteen shillings a pair. In Messrs. Green's list of prices, the African ones are two shillings less than the others. The little Avadavats are eight shillings, and so are the Silver Beaks.

5. CORDON BLUES are pretty pale blue birds, and there are Saffron Finches, or South African Canaries, and Fire Finches, of most brilliant colour, as their name implies. A collection of one pair of each of these several kinds would be fairly dazzling.

6. The CUT-THROAT SPARROWS are of rather a larger size. The cock bird has a wide crimson band just round the throat; they are very slender, beautifully marked with grey and brown, the exquisite feathers being like separate spangles; they make, however, a rather harsh sort of twittering, much like other sparrows.

The hen bird has not the bright red stripe, but she is very pretty. These birds are just the size of Goldfinches; their price, eight shillings a pair.

Indigo birds and Diamond Sparrows are each about eight to ten, and twelve to twenty shillings the pair.

7. The JAVA SPARROWS, too, are nice birds, having a sweet and liquid song, which, though it is short, is very frequent, and sometimes almost continuously repeated.

These birds are pretty, of a darkish grey plumage, as neat as it can be, black head and white cheeks, pink bills, red eyelids, and pinkish white feet. They are always pluming themselves, and caressing each other in a very loving manner. The pair I have cost ten shillings; they were from Mr. Hawkins's, and are remarkably fine. These birds greatly delight in

washing; they eat canary and millet seed, and like
wide, square perches, which should be changed very
often for fresh clean ones.

They do best, perhaps, in a bell-shaped cage with
a wooden floor, or in an aviary amidst other birds.

8. The GERMAN CANARIES are far the sweetest
singers of these very sweet voiced tribes. Their prices
range from six shillings to ten shillings and sixpence,
hens about two shillings. For those who fancy trying
their success at rearing prize Canaries, Messrs. Green
have also the thorough-bred Belgian birds, the most
prevailing, though odd-looking kind, from ten and sixpence to thirty shillings a pair—the cock and hen
of these being the same price. I have not seen their
stock, but it is said to be good, and most places have a
speciality for some sort of bird. Mr. Hawkins's, for
example, is *the* place for Mule birds. In giving
these recommendations I do not pretend to be
at all infallible, only knowing it was so difficult for
amateurs to get good birds without knowing where
to go, I took a great deal of trouble, and went to a
great deal of expense, in buying birds "promiscuously"
at all sorts of places, till I had succeeded in discovering
three or four really to be recommended.

At both Messrs. Green's and Hawkins's there is also
a large stock of cages, as good, I suppose, as any of
their respective sorts. The birds, at both these
places, are, as far as I know, invariably sent out in

first-rate condition. The foreign birds I have had at
different times from each have been good, and when
I have wanted to arrange a group, the information as
to those that might be safe to live together I have
found trustworthy, and evidently founded on a long
experience.

9. English birds I have never purchased at these
great places; it is much cheaper to buy straight from
one of the men who supplies these birds, and I, for
one, rather like the chance of getting hold of all sorts
of queer, roundabout experience of the wild birds'
ways. Litolff, of Rose Street, Long Acre, sells
English birds. It is, however, a great point in all
cases, that they should not be bought when quite
newly caught.

10. A BULLFINCH is always a favourite bird, and
uncommonly sociable. It requires rather a spacious
cage, and does very well in one of the German zinc
kind. He will much like being let out now and then
in a room, when he will sidle about and be very
funny. A common Bullfinch costs about five to seven
shillings.

11. One or two GOLDFINCHES, in a small cage,
become excessively tame, and may be let out continually. Small square cages, with the back and
top of wood, are best for them. The zinc ones they
peck more than is safe. These birds are generally
from half-a-crown to seven shillings.

12. The ROBIN REDBREAST is a pleasant bird to have flying about the room. My own has a German cage, one of the zinc bell-shaped ones, in which he lives or not as it seems good to him. Robins would not be happy if obliged to stay in a cage, though they are so very much at home in a more extended space, and go in and out of their own house. My tame Robin, too, attracts others of his own race; and I have hardly ever heard a more sweet and silvery song than that of one of these wild Robins sitting on a geranium or evergreen, and singing with all its might.

13. THRUSHES, too, are delightful birds, when we want to "make believe" that we are amongst the fields. After a summer shower, even in confinement, what a flood of melody the "mavis and merle" pour out!

14. A party of the mischievous TOM TITS should live alone, though I do not believe in their hurting other birds. A good sized bell-shaped cage shows them best, but a square one perhaps is the better for them. Their brothers, the "Joe Bents," are murderous, and must be excluded.

15. WRENS. A very small wired cage or latticed house may contain these mites of birds. They like very much, also, to fly about the room, and to sleep in warm, snug nooks. But the nooks must be very warm indeed, as they are very tender.

16. CHAFFINCHES are brisk, lively birds to have

alone. They are difficult to tame, which makes it all the pleasanter when they do become so. They may be taught to sing beautifully, having peculiarly clear sweet voices.

17. REDPOLES are excessively elegant little birds, something like Linnets, with bright red patches exactly on their foreheads.

18. LINNETS are amongst the tamest and gentlest birds for cages.

19. YELLOW HAMMERS should not be overlooked, being extremely handsome, and sometimes breeding with the Canary. The hen bird is not, however, nearly so handsome as her bright, yellow-headed mate.

20. All these English birds, and many other kinds, , can be got from Litolff, the German bird-dealer I mentioned; the prices vary from sixpence to two shillings each. Bullfinches and Thrushes fetch higher prices; the former cost from about three, the latter from four or five shillings upwards, according to time of year or scarceness. A real good Thrush or Bullfinch is by no means common. A piping Bullfinch costs from one to two guineas and upwards.

21. WANTS OF BIRDKEEPERS.—Amongst the various things that are found useful in keeping birds, I may mention first the cages; varying from the cheapest and commonest form, to the largest and most elaborate aviaries.

Of the simplest construction is a sort of cage I have used very much, because while it is excessively cheap, and handy to stow away, yet when in use it gives the birds plenty of light and air, and is easily kept clean. These are the common market cages, sold by any dealer.

There is a wooden sort of trough divided off for the seed, which is so far preferable to many of the smart cages, that the birds can get easily at their food, and a little tin hooked on, contains the supply of water. These hooked-on tins are better than water-glasses, as they are less likely to be turned aside. These cages are made of various sizes ; and I find it most handy, the doors opening at one end, to let the birds go daily from one that is dirty, into another clean one. They have slides, not drawers, and if made as I am having some done, either in stained and varnished deal, or in polished wood, they are really pretty. A tin barrel can then replace the common cup now used for the water. These cages heap together at night, and cover up in a pile in a very convenient fashion. The prices in deal and tin wire are about fourpence each for those five by six inches, sixpence for those seven by eight, and a shilling (when they are much higher) seven inches by eight.

22. I have also had made a very large cage on the same principles, three feet by eighteen inches, with a nice sort of perch for the birds to hop along, a sort

of ladder all along the bottom, four perches high up, and four more lower down alternately. A drawer goes down the middle for containing food, and another drawer runs along at the end for holding water. The perches should have deep slits for taking in and out. The cost of a mahogany cage like this is sixteen shillings; in polished deal, thirteen.

I have more than two dozen birds in one of these cages; Canaries, Goldfinches, Linnets, Greenfinches, Bullfinches, Crossbills, Yellow-hammers, Mules, and a Chaffinch. This cage being portable, and at the same time so open, affords me an immense deal of amusement.

23. For those who like the zinc and fancy cages, there are abundance to choose from at Messrs. Green's establishment, and I have found his illustrated list very useful in giving an idea of the sort of shapes there are; the prices, sizes, and fashions varying immensely. Many of the zinc and bell-cages stand on a rosewood or mahogany foundation, the tray which forms the bottom of the cage *not* being of metal. The prices of these range from four and sixpence upwards; breeding-cages, four shillings. Hospitals and baths may be made much the same, only flannel instead of wire in the one case, a dish instead of perches and seed-boxes in the other.

24. My aviary cage was made by F. Millar, Cotter's Place, Old Brompton. It cost five pounds,

when stained and varnished, in a way not in the
least injurious to the birds. The dimensions are,
four feet long, four feet high at the back, and
two feet deep. A wire shelf forms the back six
inches of the roof, and the front slopes down to
three feet from the floor. There is a wire partition which divides the cage into two equal parts,
drawing completely out, and two trays also hook upon
the wire, forming two more divisions, all entirely
separate, so that it may be one immense cage, as
large nearly as most greenhouse aviaries, or it may
make two, three, or four separate parts, each being
as large as from four to eight ordinary breeding-cages.
The sides are doors, with a secure fastening, and
these again have small doors in them to open into the
separate divisions.

The perches are large and round, and fit all along
the cage, as well as being stationed at different heights
across. They are made with a very deep cut at each
end, so that they slip backward and forward and thus
fit to the wire.

25. The seed-boxes are made sloping and with
a row of little arches for the birds to eat through,
and perches in front fixed to them. Glass or tin
pans are fitted in for seed and water; but I hope
soon these pans for birds will be made in the same
red material as the common flower-pots, glazed inside
as their saucers are.

26. Flower-pot saucers are in the meanwhile among the best of seed and water holders for standing on a cage floor, as the birds can perch upon their edges quite comfortably.

My cage has another feeder, for the inhabitants are so numerous that we need a good large dining-room. A hanging box, of much the same shape as the other, goes all along the end, containing alternately boxes of seed and water.

27. The trays draw out for cleaning, or if it is preferred to dispense with them in the breeding season, a small hoe answers every cleaning purpose.

28. The side doors are made capacious, to enable me to add large plants and branches inside. The general effect can be seen in the frontispiece.

29. I have already mentioned the importance of getting the best seed only. Ants' eggs, teasles, and thistle-seed, may be obtained from the house I mentioned as supplying English birds. The red bird sand is one penny a quart.

30. The other requisites that occur to me for bird keeping would be a tray for placing all the apparatus on, which is very useful ; a few tin canisters, or glass preserve jars, or even common bottles *without corks*, for containing the various seeds. I say, "without corks," because of the danger of any small pieces being swallowed ; glass stoppers or gutta percha ones can be used instead.

A bread-grater is essential; and if there are many birds, either a mortar or a small coffee mill is a serviceable addition. A mortar costs about a sovereign, and is hard work to pound in; a coffee mill costs three shillings, is no trouble at all, and does its work better; so I recommend the coffee mill.

A glass dish for a bath, a wire basket for suspending it in the aviary, and a sieve for sifting the seed and sand from the husks or dirt, will be also wanted. All these things, however, are matters of taste and means.

My pet Goldfinch of all lives in a sixpenny cage, and himself cost half-a-crown; living quite contentedly with his tin to drink from and his trough of seed. And as these moderate accommodations are all that are really requisite, I do not think that bird-keeping is necessarily a very expensive pleasure, whilst, of my own experience, I know it to be a great one.

THE END.

London: SMITH, ELDER & Co., Little Green Arbour Court, Old Bailey, E.C.

By the same Author,

"IN-DOOR PLANTS, AND HOW
TO GROW THEM. For the Balcony, &c."
With a Frontispiece. Uniform with "Song
Birds." 2*s.* 6*d.* cloth.

And

"FLOWERS AND FOLIAGE FOR
IN-DOOR PLANT CASES; or, Hints for arrang-
ing and preserving Flowers in Cases and in
Rooms." 1*s.* sewed.

LONDON: SMITH, ELDER & CO., 65, CORNHILL.